THE ESSENTIAL PLASTICS INDUSTRY

The Chemical Industry Education Centre was founded in 1988 as a joint venture between the Chemical Industries Association and the University of York. It is sited in the Department of Chemistry in the University.

The Centre has established a national and international reputation for its many teaching and learning resources for secondary and primary schools. *The Essential Plastics Industry* and its sister publication the *Essential Chemical Industry* are but a couple of these.

The Centre has:

- undertaken several studies of children's perceptions of industry and has developed educational activities to influence these responded to teachers' needs for up-to-date information and innovative ideas to motivate student learning through the implementation of an information service and development of teaching and learning materials

- provided, through its website and publications, activities for use in the classroom and on the manufacturing sites which enhance the curriculum.

CIEC also has an information service which responds speedily to enquiries from teachers and their students on a huge range of subjects about the industry.

The Centre arranges training for companies, organisations which link industry and education such as Education Business Link Organisations, Local Education Authorities, schools and for the Association for Science Education, ASE.

In all this work, the Centre aims to enhance the effective teaching of science and technology by enthusing students and generating a better understanding of the respective needs of schools and industry.

Authors: Mike Driver, James Pitt

Editors: Valmai Firth, James Pitt, Miranda Stephenson

Chemical Industry Education Centre
University of York

The team is grateful for the work of Amanda Finch,
Heidi Allene Henrickson and Alison Penny who helped
source many of the photographs in the publication.

THE ESSENTIAL PLASTICS INDUSTRY

Published by:

Chemical Industry Education Centre,
University of York,
York, YO10 5DD, UK
Tel: 01904 432523
e-mail: ciec@york.ac.uk

www.ciec.org.uk

First edition: 2003

ISBN: 1 85342 581 8

Design: Barry Perks Design, York
Prepared and printed in England by: Colorworks Print Ltd

Brief descriptions of the polymers found in this
publication and how they are manufactured.

ATOFINA, the chemical branch of the Oil Group TotalFinaElf, was created in April 2000 from the merger of the chemical and petrochemical activities of TotalFina and Elf Aquitaine.

With over 70,000 employees and sales of some €20 bn in 2001, **ATOFINA** is one of the major chemical companies in the world.

ATOFINA chemicals enjoy leading positions both in Europe and in the World in each of the Company's three core activities:

Petrochemicals and Commodity Polymers
> Olefins, Aromatics, Polyethylene, Polypropylene, Styrenics, Fertilisers, PVC.

Intermediates and Performance Polymers
> Chlorochemicals, Acrylics, Fluorochemicals and Oxygenated Products, Organic Peroxides, Thiochemicals, Plastic Additives, Engineering and Functional Polymers.

Specialty Chemicals
> Rubber products for the automotive, aerospace and consumer sectors, Paints and Coatings, Adhesives and Electroplating products.

With operations on all five continents, particularly in Europe, North America and Asia, **ATOFINA** is a dedicated partner to many industrial sectors in diverse markets ranging from automotive and transport, packaging, construction and civil engineering through to sports and leisure, health, hygiene and beauty, water, paper, electronics, agriculture, etc.

In line with **ATOFINA**'s Environmental Policy, the company is committed to the guiding principles of Sustainable Development, ensuring that every aspect of its operations is carried out with the highest regard to public health and the world around us.

The Essential Plastics Industry was first published in 1997 under the title *Understanding Plastics*. The name of this publication has changed and so has the name of its sponsor, from Elf Atochem to ATOFINA. Names may change, the content may be updated, but what remains is a fundamental need: to inform and motivate young people to empathise with one of our essential industries, the Plastics Industry.

The original idea for *Understanding Plastics* came from the success of a similar publication in France, sponsored by our parent company. There were many modifications and improvements, however, and what started out as essentially a translation of an existing French document became a user friendly text largely re-written to meet the needs of A-level and advanced GNVQ candidates in Britain. This latest edition – *The Essential Plastics Industry* – is again so very different from the original that it deserves the name change that highlights the indispensable role that plastics play in our 21st century lives.

This book is published as a sister book to *The Essential Chemical Industry*, also produced by CIEC, the Chemical Industry Education Centre, a joint initiative of The University of York and the Chemical Industries Association. ATOFINA is indebted to CIEC, without whose hands-on work this edition of The Essential Plastics Industry would not have been published. It is one thing to find a solution to a perceived need, it is another to bring it from concept to reality. We are also grateful to The Plastics Committee of the Worshipful Company of Horners for their research and proof reading of the text.

This publication will have succeeded in its objectives if the properties and merits of plastic materials are more widely appreciated. ATOFINA is delighted to be involved in this initiative and wishes students reading this book much success in the future.

D.P. Gresham
Chairman & Managing Director
ATOFINA UK Ltd.

ACKNOWLEDGMENTS

In each of the companies and organisations we have consulted, individuals have given us their expertise and experience, often far beyond that which we have the right to expect.

adidas
APME (Association of Plastics Manufacturers in Europe)
British Plastics Federation
Cannon Rubber Ltd
Dunlop Slazenger
Dyson Ltd
Ford
GE Plastics
GlaxoSmithKline
Harkness Hall UK
ITDG (Intermediate Technology Development Group)
Nicholas Grimshaw and Partners Ltd
Nuffield Design and Technology
PDD
PP Global Technology
Priestman Goode
Rapak (D S Smith Plastics)
Seymour Powell
Skystreme
smart™ (DaimlerChrysler UK)
St Paul's Nursery School, York
Symphony Environmental Ltd
The British Council
The Design Council
The Eden Project
The Fabric University
UCB Group
Wolfson Electrostatics
Worshipful Company of Horners

Special thanks to:

John Amner, Ivor Davies, David Egglestone, John Featherstone, Mandy Haberman, Bernie Hanning, Denny Lane, David Oxley, John Sale, Colin Williamson

Our grateful thanks also to ATOFINA for their very generous financial support.

We also thank for following companies and organisations for giving us permission to use photographs. The numbers refer to the pages on which they can be found.

adidas, 70
Aesculap AG and Company KG, 20
Amanda Penny, 85
Arcadia Group, 48
Apex Photo Agency Limited, 34
ATOFINA, 19, 52, 55, 61, 62, 73, 75, 76, 77, 88, 91, 108, 113, 115
AVENT, Cannon Rubber Limited, 40, 41
BASF, 69
Board-a-Line Limited, 32, 33
Cambridge Display Technology Limited, 17
City of York Council, 11
DaimlerChrysler, 63
Dan Gavere, 101
DuPont, 51, 69
Dyson, 72
Elizabeth Hubbard, 85
Erhard & Söhne GmbH, 11
Freefoto.com, 27
Gilbert, 54
GlaxoSmithKline, 55
Graham Johnson, NSW Agriculture, 9
Graham Hearn, Wolfson Electrostatics, 12
Graham Mathers 4, 8, 9, 19, 21, 22, 27, 39, 43, 64, 66, 68, 84, 85, 91, 92, 94, 96, 97, 99, 102
Hemera Technologies Incorporated, 18, 27, 43, 67, 101, 104
Horners Company, 20, 21
Hugh Craig Harpsichords, 79
Hutchison Picture Library, 30
James Pitt, 19, 28, 36, 43, 47, 48, 67, 72, 83, 85, 87, 101
Kath James, 35
Kelvin Fagan, 69
Koninklijke Philips Electronics NV, 18
Larson Boats, 80, 103
Lucite International, 87
Mandy Haberman, 41, 42
Microban International Limited, 17
Mothercare, 39
National Museum of Photography, Film & Television, 28, 78
Negri Bossi, 93
NetMotion Incorporated (info@netmotion.com), 19
Plastics Historical Society, 113
Priestman Goode, 59
Robert Speht Energy Tech Limited (http://www.energytech.co.uk), 5
Roger Ferragallo, 79
RPT Company, 19
Salomon Sports, 53
Samsonite, 59
Sanford, 68
Seymour Powell Design, 29
Shell UK, 22, 117
Skystreme UK Limited, 86
Sony, 47
Sossna GmbH, 108
Stanmore Implants Worldwide Limited, 87
The Centre for Alternative Technology, 4
Tripleplas, 100
UCB Films, 30
University of Leicester, 39
University of York, 28
Wacky Wet World, 71

PLASTICS - MATERIALS FOR A SUSTAINABLE FUTURE?

PLASTICS -
MATERIALS FOR A SUSTAINABLE FUTURE?

Civilisation does not stand still. Every year there are changes to the way we live, the products we use, the systems through which society is organised. One only needs to consider the impact of computers and mobile phones as products, and the Internet and telephone cellular networks as systems, to see how changing technologies and life-styles interact.

But do all changes make life better? Are we sometimes meeting needs now in a way that will create problems for future generations? Are the choices being made today limiting the chance of people in the future to meet their needs?

These are the questions that underlie the concept of *sustainable development*. The simplest definition is that development (or change) is sustainable if it meets the needs of today without compromising the ability of future generations to meet their needs. Sustainability is essentially about choices. If governments, companies or individuals commit irreversible acts, such as cutting down forests or releasing toxic chemicals, this reduces the choices of future generations.

Sustainable development is now a policy priority at all levels – the United Nations, international agencies such as The World Bank, individual governments, companies and NGOs (non-governmental organisations) – all have policies on sustainable development. They do not always live up to these policies, but at least the question of sustainable change is becoming central to their thinking.

This is a book about plastics. To what extent have plastic products and the industries that lie behind them, contributed towards sustainable development? To answer this, we need first to examine the concept more closely.

1.1 Sustainability is a direction of travel, not a destination

There is no such thing as a truly sustainable product, be it made from a plastic or another material! What is more important is whether the new or redesigned product is *more sustainable than the product it is replacing*.

Consider plastic bags being used at supermarkets. These have replaced paper bags. Are they more sustainable? In some ways they are. They are far lighter and thinner, thus the transport costs and environmental pollution incurred in getting them from factory to shop is less. They *can* be used again and again. They *can* be collected and recycled or burned to create heat. But *are* they? Better collection, sorting and recycling facilities would enhance the sustainability of the move from paper to plastic carrier bags. But there are also negative consequences of this development. Most plastics are made from oil, which is a finite resource. They require energy intensive processing. Toxins can be released. And we all know how plastic carrier bags can

litter roadsides, get caught in trees, and remain for decades in landfill sites.

But when we think about the issue more, it is not so straightforward. The manufacture of paper carrier bags certainly uses a renewable source (trees). If we consider the energy used over the whole life cycle of the bag, it does not compare well with the plastic alternative. Papermaking is not without its toxic problems. And is the real problem not so much the product, but the behaviour of the people who use it? After all, people create litter, not plastics manufacturers. Whether or not there are good collection and recycling facilities is a matter of choice, which is of course affected by economics. Collection points exist in some countries, for example Germany, or in some parts of Britain, but not in others.

All these questions can be asked about many other plastic products. So is a society that is making greater use of plastic products moving towards more sustainable living? On balance, we would argue that given the right infrastructure, the development towards plastic products is a move in the right direction, that is, plastics can contribute to sustainable development. But there is more to this issue than simple environmental impact. One needs to look at economic and social factors to get a balanced picture.

1.2 The different facets of sustainable development

There are three main dimensions to sustainable development – environmental, social and economic. Three interlocking circles can represent them:

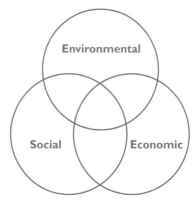

When analysing the impact of a new product, material, processing technology or system, it is helpful to use these three broad headings. It is not enough to simply say that a product is good or bad. We need more subtle tools for analysis.

The Total Beauty of Sustainable Products is the name of a book by philosopher and design guru Edwin Datschefski. In it he describes five simple tests for sustainability – cyclic, solar, safe, efficient, social. We will add another – economic. The questions overlap to some extent.

PLASTICS -
MATERIALS FOR A SUSTAINABLE FUTURE?

But this simply reflects the synergy between the three dimensions of sustainable development. The descriptions below describe an ideal we are working towards. In some cases the goal may not be achievable.

1.2.1. Is it cyclic?

This phrase 'Is it cyclic?' is a short-hand way to ask is the product made from compostable, organic materials, or from minerals that can be continuously recycled in a 'closed loop'?

The idea here is that there should be no such thing as waste! All by-products should be the 'raw material' for something else. Metals can be recycled again and again. Something that really has to be thrown away might be burned to release the energy stored in it. Or it can be put into compost, to provide nutrients for the soil. In this way, carbon and nitrogen can be recycled.

> "We've often heard that we're running out of resources. But there are still the same number of atoms around on the earth's surface – we have simply converted atoms into molecules that are of no use to us. With continuous cycling of both organic and inorganic materials, we will never run out of the resources we need."
>
> Edwin Datschefski

1.2.2 Is it solar?

In manufacture and use, do the products consume only renewable energy that is cyclic and safe?

We can use energy directly from the sun through photovoltaic cells and through using other types of solar panels. Energy comes indirectly from the sun in wave and wind power, hydro-electricity, and biomass (energy stored in plants) (see Boxes 1.1, 1.2 & 1.3)

> "Each day more solar energy falls to the earth than the total amount of energy the planet's 6 billion inhabitants would consume in 25 years. We've hardly begun to tap the potential of solar energy"
>
> US Department of Energy –
> quoted by Edwin Datschefski

Box 1.1 Fully biodegradable plastics from sustainable sources

New plastics are being developed that can be made from organic chemicals obtained from renewable resources such as corn or wheat. An example is polylactic acid, PLA. The starch produced by photosynthesis in the plant is first separated and is then converted into dextrose sugar. This is in turn converted to lactic acid using a fermentation process. A cyclic dimer is formed using a condensation reaction. This is purified using vacuum distillation and is then polymerised in a reaction where the lactide ring opens up forming a polymer PLA. This polymer can be used to make a range of items including clothing, home and office furnishings, cups, food containers and sweet wrappers. It is hoped to be able to make bottles also. Claims have been made that the production of PLA consumes 20%-30% less fossil fuel than comparable plastics derived from crude oil.

Box 1.2 The use of plastics in capturing solar energy

Solar energy, of course, needs to be captured. Plastics are used in the manufacture of solar panels and wind turbines.

Solar energy can be converted directly into electrical energy using photovoltaic cells, which are made from plastics. Solar energy is particularly valuable in remote areas, which are not served by a national electrical grid. This applies to about 2 million people worldwide.

For examaple, a Regional Solar Program (PRS), the most ambitious one undertaken by the European Union, will provide power for 330 water pumping stations, 240 community lighting systems, 63 refrigeration services and 36 battery recharging stations in remote regions of Africa. This solar technology will ensure the availability of clean drinking water and provide reliable crop irrigation and community electrical services.

PLASTICS -
MATERIALS FOR A SUSTAINABLE FUTURE?

Box 1.3 Wind Power

Wind power is now the world's fastest growing energy source and is a rapidly expanding industry. Plastics are used in the manufacture of wind turbines. During the 1990's wind energy capacity expanded at an annual rate of 25.7%, doubling every 3 years. The American Wind Energy Association report that in 1999 global wind energy capacity exceeded 10 000 megawatts - enough to serve over 5 cities the size of Miami. This is equivalent to the energy from 34 million barrels of oil. A report from the California Energy Commission in 1996 compares the cost of wind energy favourable with other sources of energy. This calculates the levelised costs of various sources of energy. Levelised costs include all capital, fuel and operating and maintenance costs associated with the plant over its lifetime, and divides that total cost by the estimated output in kWh over the lifetime of the plant. Plastics are used in the construction of wind turbines and are therefore contributing to the conservation of other fuels.

Fuel	Levelised costs (cents/kWh) (1996)
Coal	4.8-5.5
Gas	3.9-4.4
Hydroelectric	5.1-11.3
Biomass	5.8-11.6
Nuclear	11.1-14.5
Wind	4.0-6.0

Source California Energy Commission 1996 Energy Technology Status Report.

The cost of natural gas has increased since 1996 meaning that the levelised costs of gas-fired plants would be higher. It should also be noted that the costs given above do not include any environmental costs. If these were included then wind energy would be even more competitive.

Source: website of American Wind Energy Association (http//:www.awea.org)

1.2.3 Is it safe?

Are all releases to air, water, land or space the raw materials for other systems?

A safe product or process is one that does not harm other people or life, physically or chemically. You need to consider the whole life cycle (see Box 1.4) of the product:

- the extraction of raw materials
- the materials themselves
- the manufacturing processes
- all transport involved
- the impact of distribution, sale
- use (and misuse!)
- and the ultimate 'disposal' of the product.

A totally safe product generates nothing harmful, nor any waste, at any stage. We need also to think of the social impact of the product or process under the heading of safety – see section 1.2.5, page 9.

PLASTICS -
MATERIALS FOR A SUSTAINABLE FUTURE?

Box 1.4 Life Cycle Analysis

The choice of material for a given application is based on a large number of criteria. First of all, the material must comply with the specifications, which define parameters such as appearance, sturdiness, shape, etc. Secondly, the cost is a paramount factor, particularly in relation to the product's end-use. Finally, the impact of the use of a given material on the environment is now increasingly taken into consideration.

The impact on the environment may be broken down as follows:

- energy consumption (non-renewable resource)

- air pollution

- water pollution

- soil pollution (solid waste).

A variety of techniques are used to assess this impact, including a method known as 'life cycle analysis'.

Life cycle analysis consists of evaluating the consequences on the environment of an essential human activity and making judgements on the various ways available to fulfil this activity, for example choice of materials, processes, waste management methods, etc.

A number of issues have to be taken into account for this type of analysis to be made.

The first step consists of compiling data to quantify both direct and indirect nuisances. For example, when a product requires electrical energy for its manufacture, the analysis must include effects on the environment of:

- extracting crude oil, gas or coal, for use in the power station

- operating a power station

- the impact from the plant which is manufacturing the product.

The second step looks into the manufacture of the product, and goes on to consider the consequences of both use and disposal at the end of the product's life.

A complete picture of a product's impact on the environment requires an assessment of its entire life and not just the end of its life.

Life cycle analysis is carried out in four different stages:

1) The objectives of the life cycle analysis project are defined.

2) An 'Ecobalance' or Life Cycle Inventory establishes a quantitative inventory of:

 - energy consumption

 - use of raw materials

 - emissions into the environment (water, air, waste). A Life Cycle Inventory examines all the processes involved, from raw material extraction to waste disposal.

3) Through impact analysis a quantitative relationship between the inventory and the effects on the environment (energy consumption, air pollution, water pollution, waste, etc.) is established.

4) Through a systematic study of strong points, as well as weak points, and the assessment of potential ways of reducing environmental drawbacks, a plan for improvement is drawn up. This will involve listing which areas for improvement are priorities.

This publication does not feature a complete study of the problem. The following case, which examines energy consumption - a major facet of life cycle analysis - is just one example of this type of environmental study.

PLASTICS - MATERIALS FOR A SUSTAINABLE FUTURE?

Box 1.4 continued

Example: car wing

Step 1

a)   Objectives defined

Manufacture, use over 150 000 km and possible recycling or energy recovery at end of life. Based on the following options:

- plastic wing weighing 2.5 kg
- aluminium wing weighing 2.9 kg
- steel wing weighing 5.3 kg.

Step 2 & 3

b)   Ecobalance and Impact Analysis

Both the use and the transportation of goods which are intended to travel long distances, such as automotive components, or collected waste, are fundamental factors in the ecobalance. In this example, plastic wings, which initially require less energy during manufacture than aluminium or steel wings, also offer, by virtue of their lower weight, the biggest energy savings during their transportation and their actual use over 150 000 km (see table below).

Step 4

c)   Improvement Analysis

Logically, therefore, this analysis favours an increased use of plastic components instead of steel whenever technically feasible. This will lead to reduced energy consumption during the manufacture of cars and, above all, during their use, with the additional benefit of less traffic-related air pollution.

In many cases, the impact of plastics on the environment is less severe than that of other materials. In terms of increased protection of the environment, they are appropriate materials to consider as substitutes.

Consumption (+) and/or Energy savings (-)	Energy impact in litre fuel equivalent*		
	Plastic wing (2.5 kg)	Aluminium wing (2.9 kg)	Steel wing (5.3 kg)
For manufacture of wing	6	21	7
For making it 'run' over 150 000 km	18	21	38
Energy recovered from recycling it	-1	-14	-2
Total	23	28	43

*1 litre of fuel is taken as being equal to 40 MJ (round figures).

Source: Plastics, Rubber and Composites Processing and Applications, Vol. 16, no.3, 1991

PLASTICS -
MATERIALS FOR A SUSTAINABLE FUTURE?

1.2.4 Is it efficient?

Every product requires energy, materials and water for its production and use. We need to reduce our use of these resources. Can an equivalent or better product be produced with less (see Box 1.5)?

In the long term, is the product economic to make? Or does it create problems that someone else will have to pay for in the future?

Box 1.5 Energy Saving

The use of plastics for insulation in buildings, and the lightness of plastic packaging and automobile components, is reducing the amount of energy required for heating and transport.

Energy calculations show that using plastics for food packaging can result in energy **savings** that are over twice the energy needed to produce, fill and transport the packaging. This saves resources.

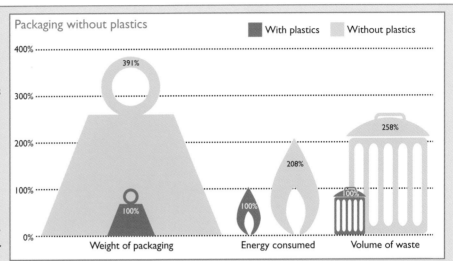

Plastics are often **energy efficient** compared to other packaging materials. This is shown quite dramatically by the results of a German study in 1991.

In fact, since the German study, the energy efficiency of plastics has increased further. This has been achieved by reducing the weight and the thickness of packaging. Over a 10-year period, from 1988-1997, the weight of the average plastics package was reduced by 28%, saving 3 million tonnes of plastic and reducing the weight of plastics waste. Between 40 - 50% of goods in Europe are packaged using plastics. The total weight of plastics packaging is, however, only 10% of all packaging and plastics waste forms less than 1% of Europe's waste by weight. 40% of plastic waste is currently recovered and this will increase.

Poly(phenylethene), PS, packaging

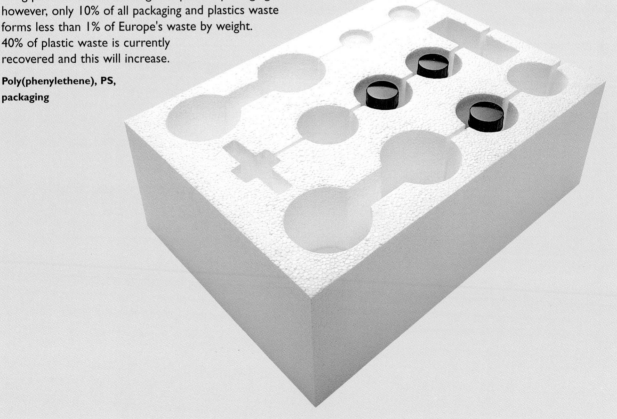

PLASTICS -
MATERIALS FOR A SUSTAINABLE FUTURE?

1.2.5 Is it social?

Do the manufacture and use of the product support basic human rights and natural justice?

Are the working conditions safe and compatible with human dignity? Are people paid properly at all stages of the supply chain? Does the product reinforce equality of opportunity? Does it enhance cultural diversity? Does it encourage participation in society?

It is not easy to answer these broad questions for most products. But there are some direct ways in which plastics can improve the quality of life, for example in the preservation and distribution of food and water in an economic and reliable manner (see Boxes 1.6 & 1.7).

Box 1.6 Conserving Water
The use of plastics to conserve water

In regions of the world where there is a lack of water there is a need to conserve existing water and use irrigation systems to distribute it. Plastics are chosen for many of these applications because they are low cost, hard-wearing, easy to transport and assemble. For potable water supplies the pipes are non-toxic and non-tainting i.e. do not impart effluent or odour to the water carried.

The lightness of the plastic is important in areas of the world where the terrain is difficult and the only form of transport is by foot. WaterAid is a charity which concentrates on providing water supplies, together with sanitation and hygiene promotion in the developing world. Plastic piping has enabled WaterAid to bring clean water supplies to over 7 million people in the developing world.

Box 1.7 Conserving Food

The use of plastics to conserve food

In Europe the level of food wastage is approximately 2%. This is partly due to the use of plastic packaging.

About 60% of plastics packaging is used in packaging food. Plastics packaging materials have a valuable range of properties: low weight, ease of moulding, barrier properties, strength, shatter resistance and transparency. Plastics packaging is cost-effective and hygienic. Transparent packaging has the benefit that people can see the food but cannot touch it. Food products are perishable and plastics packaging seals in freshness and nutritional value. The use of plastics for packaging also helps to prevent food poisoning, which can result when juices from raw meat, fish or poultry come into contact with other foods.

In recent years further advances have been made in packaging which maintain the taste and nutritional value of food at a high level. For example special multi-layer plastics films have been developed which will keep fish fresh for two days when stored in the normal self-service cooling systems of supermarkets. This development is useful because fish is very sensitive under normal atmospheric conditions and is difficult to keep fresh.

In the developing areas of the world the rate of food wastage is about 50%.

1.2.6 Is it economic?

This question overlaps with the idea of efficiency – the more efficiently something is produced in terms of energy, materials and water, the more economic it is. It also overlaps with the social questions. But there are other questions. Does production and use of the product create jobs that are sustainable? Is there a net increase in decently paid jobs where they are needed?

PLASTICS -
MATERIALS FOR A SUSTAINABLE FUTURE?

1.3 How do these questions relate to the three dimensions of sustainability?

The diagram below shows how these six questions relate to the different dimensions of sustainability. For example, the question of safety can be asked both about releases into the environment, and in terms of the safe working conditions of people involved in manufacture or further down the supply chain. The issue of sustainable job creation is both a social and an economic issue.

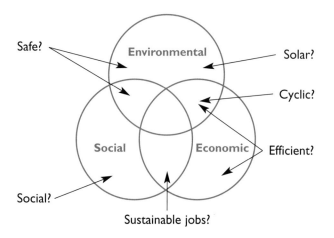

A product might be a step forward in one dimension but not so good in another. For example:

- Collecting, sorting and recycling plastic bottles might create jobs and reduce waste emissions (good in the social and environmental dimensions) – but not be economically viable on a local level.

- A car can be developed which uses fuel more efficiently, by using recyclable and recycled plastics to reduce its weight and generally having has less materials in it (steps forward in the economic and environmental dimensions) – but what is the social effect of more and more cars in use? Might it not be better to concentrate on improving public transport?

Box 1.8: Plastic waste as a proportion of total waste West Europe - 1999

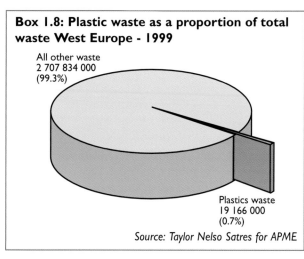

All other waste
2 707 834 000
(99.3%)

Plastics waste
19 166 000
(0.7%)

Source: Taylor Nelso Satres for APME

Box 1.9: Plastics recovery in Western Europe 2000 (x 1000 tonnes)

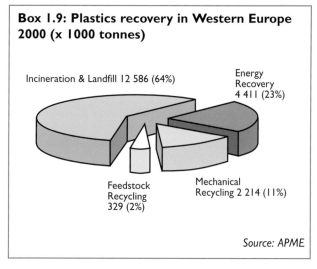

Incineration & Landfill 12 586 (64%)

Energy Recovery 4 411 (23%)

Feedstock Recycling 329 (2%)

Mechanical Recycling 2 214 (11%)

Source: APME

Box 1.10: Plastics recovery

	Recycling (%)	Energy recovery (%)	Unrecovered waste (%)
Austria*	19	22	59
Belgium	18	27	55
Denmark	7	75	18
Finland	14	19	67
France	8	32	60
Germany*	29	26	45
Greece	2	19	79
Ireland	7	0	93
Italy	11	9	80
Netherlands	15	59	26
Portugal	3	24	73
Spain	14	7	79
Sweden	10	43	47
United Kingdom	7	6	87
Total EU	13	20	67
Norway	15	43	42
Switzerland	7	73	20
Western Europe	13	23	64

* Recycling in Germany and Austria includes 346 000 tonnes via feedstock recycling.
All figures rounded to nearest %
Source: APME

PLASTICS -
MATERIALS FOR A SUSTAINABLE FUTURE?

1.4 The Effective Management of Waste Plastics

In Western Europe, the total of all plastics waste is less than one per cent of all waste by weight (see Box 1.8). Plastics packaging waste is just over half the total of this post- plastics waste. Whilst the percentage is very small, the actual amount of waste (approximately 9.5 million tonnes) is obviously significant.

There are two main recovery routes available for managing waste plastics - **material recycling** and **energy recovery**. Over the last few years **feedstock recycling** has also begun: at present it is operational only in Germany and Austria (see Box 1.9).

The table in Box 1.10 gives the details by country. As you will see there is a wide variation between individual countries with Denmark being top with a total recovery of 82%. Ireland is bottom with a total recovery of 7%.

1.4.1 Material Recovery

a. Mechanical Recycling

This involves reprocessing plastics by physical means to make new plastic items. Whilst most plastics can be recycled in theory, in reality there are limitations

because of the practicalities of waste collection, that is, the volume of waste, the homogeneity of the waste and how clean it is.

- *Volume* Normally products weighing less than 20g would not be considered for recycling. The very lightweight of packaging films, for example, makes them difficult to collect. In the case of the films used to wrap chocolate bars over 1 500 would be needed to make up 1 kg. Collection can be facilitated in a number of ways e.g. the use of 'voluntary waste banks' and 'second rubbish bins'.

- *Homogeneity* If plastic waste is homogeneous, that is of a single type, this makes reprocessing much easier. Where the waste consists of mixed plastics then it is necessary to sort it. This may involve some manual sorting together with use of flotation methods, which separate different plastics by means of their different densities. Automatic methods of sorting plastics are also being developed.

- *Cleanliness* If plastics waste is dirty then the process of washing it can consume almost as much energy as manufacturing virgin plastics.

Recycling bins at Dusseldorf airport.

Voluntary Waste Bank. *Picture courtesy of City of York Council*

PLASTICS -
MATERIALS FOR A SUSTAINABLE FUTURE?

Identifying plastics

The European Union is doing much to promote recyling. For example there is a directive on scrapping cars (see Box 1.11), that will lead to a new type of scrap dealer (see Box 1.12).

Box 1.11 End of Life Vehicles Directive

New laws on scrapping old cars

The EU *End of Life Vehicles Directive* was published in 2000. It required that member states have in place both legislation and an ELV disposal infrastructure by April 2002.

The Directive aims to ensure that

- All new vehicles have improved recyclability through restricting the use of hazardous materials, designing for easy disassembly, and using more recycled material.

- All existing vehicles are disposed of in an environmentally acceptable manner through removing all fluids, air-bags and anything else that is hazardous, prior to dismantling or shredding. This has to be done at a specially authorised place, which can then issue a 'Certificate of Destruction' for each vehicle.

- The amount of material that goes from the ELV shredding into landfill is reduced from 25% (2001) to 15% (2006) and ultimately to 5% (2015). This can be done by more recycling of non-metallic materials, and more energy recovery through incineration.

Box 1.12 Scrap Dealers

New scrap merchants

We are likely to see a new breed of scrap merchants, or 'Authorised Treatment Facilities'. These will be carefully controlled areas, with impermeable surfaces, secure storage facilities and a certified environmental management system. When a vehicle comes in for destruction, it will first be de-polluted by removal of all fluids – fuel, oil, anti-freeze and screen-wash. Batteries and components with mercury will be removed, as will air-bag charges. Then the tyres, glass and larger plastic components will be stripped off to aid recycling.

Ford, one of the leading automotive manufacturers when it comes to thinking recycling, already has its new cars 85% recyclable, and aims to increase this to nearer 90%. All plastic components in their new cars are already marked to show from which plastic they are made. But this is not true for all cars, and certainly not for many older cars. Also, the markings may not be easy to read, after a crash for example.

How to identify unmarked plastics?

A successful plastics recycling strategy requires that parts can be removed easily, and easily identified at the treatment facilities. This is essential to avoid cross-contamination of recycled plastics by mixing them inadvertently.

The Tribopen

Ford, in conjunction with Wolfson Electrostatics at the University of Southampton, have developed the Tribopen to make plastics identification easier. This is a simple hand-held device, with a snap-on head, that can be brushed over a plastic object. Depending on the material of the head and the material being tested, a positve or negative electrostatic charge appears, thereby lighting up a red or green LED on the pen. It can be used by an unskilled operative, either with a single pen or with several pens for more detailed sorting. The picture below shows it being used on a food container. In 2002 the Tribopen retailed at about £900.

Engineers at the University of Southampton have a working laboratory model of a conveyor belt, with a number of Tribopens fitted above it. Unsorted articles are tipped in, and as they brush past the pens, they are identified as being polyamides, PA, poly(methyl(methacrylate), PMMA, acrylonitrite-butadiene-styrene, ABS, metal, poly(propene), PP, poly(chloroethene), PVC, poly(ethene), PP or 'other'. The Tribopen sensors are linked via a computer to actuators, which then phyically sort the objects into containers. The University of Southampton anticipate that this sorting system will be developed on a commercial scale in the near future.

PLASTICS - MATERIALS FOR A SUSTAINABLE FUTURE?

Using spectography to identify plastics – the Polyana

A more sophisticated plastics identification device (also developed by the University of Southampton) is the Polyana. This is based on a redesigned spectrometer that redirects the beam outside the unit. The operator places the unidentified object against a nozzle at the front of the unit where it is hit by the measuring beam. The resulting spectrum is then compared with over 150 in the computer library, and the plastic identified together with any fillers and mixers. The software also gives the degree of certainty that the plastic has been identified correctly.

b. Feedstock Recycling

This is a type of recovery that is more suited to mixed plastic waste. The plastics are broken down into reusable monomers, chemical intermediates or synthesis gases. At present this type of chemical recycling is mainly at the development stage. In Italy there is a plant, owned by Solvay, which converts waste poly(chloroethene), PVC, to hydrochloric acid.

1.4.2 Energy Recovery

Plastics are made generally from chemicals obtained from crude oil. Like fractions from oil that can be used as fuels, so plastics can be burnt and used as a source of energy. This is a viable option where efficient mechanical recycling is not possible. Waste plastic is burnt in an efficient incinerator designed to recover energy and remove toxic and undesirable fumes. The combustion takes place at temperatures in excess of 850°C. The resulting slag and grate ash are recovered at the bottom of the furnace and can be used in the foundation materials in road construction once any residual metals have been stabilised.

The heat released is used to produce steam at high pressure. This passes through a turbine to produce electricity. Low pressure steam escapes from the turbine. Often the energy from the low pressure vapour is used to produce hot water or steam which can be distributed to industry and the community. The gaseous effluent is purified before discharge. The main pollutants are sulphur dioxide, nitrogen oxides and hydrochloric acid. These are all acidic gases and are neutralised, typically by passage through limewater. Incineration of plastics is sometimes criticised because of the release of dioxins. The latest incinerators release 1 nanogramme of dioxin per cubic metre of air released. These incinerators destroy more of the dioxins that come in with the waste than they release through combustion.

There are 275 Energy From Waste (EFW) plants in Europe, handling 47 million tonnes of waste annually and recovering 43 000 giga Watt hours of energy.

1.5 Plastics industry and sustainable development – an overview

The questions in Box 1.13 highlight the essential ambiguity of all technological change. It is very unusual if a development is wholly positive or negative. Students who use this book – whether they are studying chemistry, design & technology or general studies – will find materials to help them explore the impact of the plastics industry that has become so essential to our everyday lives.

One of the mantras of sustainable development is the three Rs' - 'Reduce - Reuse - Recycle'. Can more be made with less (materials, energy consumption, toxic releases)? Can the product or some of its components be reused, rather than replaced? Can the materials be recycled when the product is no longer useful? These are questions that every designer should consider when developing a new or improved product.

More radical thinkers add a fourth 'R' to the 'trinity' of Reduce - Reuse - Recycle that characterises sustainable living, the notion that we can refuse to buy or use a product in the first place. Should we be developing more sustainable cars? Or try to develop public transport systems that reduce the need for cars? Should we be developing packaging with less embodied energy, or use less packaging? How far do developments in plastic technology help, or hinder, moves to more sustainable living?

The overall view of the authors is that plastics do contribute towards sustainable development, but that their use needs to be more judicious, and that much remains to be done at a political and economic level to enhance the sustainability of plastics development. But it is up to you, the student, to inform and make your own judgement.

We hope that you will have both the tools for analysis, as well as useful data and sources of information. In addition it is worth visiting the web site of Recoup (http://www.recoup.org/) which will give you a portal into issues surrounding recycling plastics.

Environmental groups such as Friends of the Earth (http://www.foe.co.uk/) or Greenpeace (http://www.greenpeace.org/) can provide a first point of call for campaigns and information on environmental issues.

Organisations such as the British Plastics Federation (http://www.bpf.co.uk/) and the Association of European Plastics Manufacturers (http://www.apme.org/) have useful sites that reflect the industries' viewpoint.

PLASTICS - MATERIALS FOR A SUSTAINABLE FUTURE?

Box 1.13 Overview	Steps forward	Issues
Environmental protection	The industry is constantly striving to find ways in which to help conserve valuable resources, such as oil and fossil fuels, and to reduce the levels of the greenhouse gas CO_2 in the atmosphere. The use of plastics plays an important part in the effective distribution of water and food, and in the preservation of food. Plastics are being used more efficiently in that less is used to do more, e.g. the use of lightweight plastic packaging. There is much more activity on the recycling front – e.g. in the automotive industry. More biodegradable plastics are being developed.	Until there is much more recycling, the plastics industry still relies on oil as a raw material. What is the net environmental impact of introducing a new plastic product into the market (compared to the product it is replacing)? Many people are careless in disposing of plastics, and there are insufficient recycling schemes in place.
Economic development	The chemical industry, of which the plastics industry is part, is the second largest business sector in the European Union. Over 1 million workers are employed in Western Europe in the plastics industry: thus it makes a significant contribution to employment and wealth creation. The annual turnover is about 135 billion euros. New possibilities of plastics processing leads to innovatory products and technologies that can increase competitiveness in the market. The development of recycling facilities and processes will lead to the creation of jobs.	Just because something can be done at a profit does not mean it should be done! What sorts of jobs are created with the plastics industry? Does the capital-intensive processing industry make it almost impossible for SMEs (small to medium-sized enterprises) to compete? Is there a necessary concentration of jobs? What is the real long-term cost of disposing of plastics that are no longer needed?
Social progress	The industry contributes to improving the quality of life for all through access to better healthcare and education. Plastics play a crucial role in that many hi-tech products such as computers and mobile phones rely on plastics – communications are better today than ever before. Plastic products also enable advances to made in healthcare, comfortable transport, sports, and clothing – almost any aspect of life.	Does the availability of products always benefit human development? For example, are computer games helping or inhibiting a child's learning? Are fashionable clothes, accessories and products – many of which rely on plastics – contributing towards a 'must-have' culture that increases social division? Does the widespread availability of certain products reduce cultural diversity?

INTRODUCTION TO PLASTICS

INTRODUCTION TO PLASTICS

2.1 What characterises plastics?

People often say objects are 'made of plastic', but in fact there are many different types of plastic. Plastics are substances that can be shaped (moulded) by the use of heat and pressure. Some common examples are poly(ethene), PE (the common name is polythene), poly(chloroethene), PVC and poly(propene), PP, (polypropylene). The properties of different plastics vary from one another because of differences in their molecular formulae and molecular structures. The chemistry of common plastics covered in many examination courses can be found in Chapter 9.

Plastic materials are often associated with cheap, inferior substitutes. This impression was created because plastics were introduced as replacements for natural materials as a result of wartime shortages. The uses to which plastics were then put were not always appropriate and this created an unfavourable impression of their value. In reality, provided that they are used appropriately, plastics are very valuable materials. They can have significant advantages over natural materials and, for certain applications, plastics are the only materials that meet the requirements (see Boxes 2.1 & 2.2.)

Box 2.2 Sustainable active microbial, SAM polymers

A new range of environmentally friendly anti-microbial polyamides, PAs has been produced. These can protect surfaces against various bacteria, fungi and algae. The anti-microbial activity of the polymers is thought to be due to the charge on the nitrogen atoms in the polymer. The polymers have a potentially wide range of applications including food processing, drinking water treatment and protection of historic artefacts.

Petri dish without Microban   **Petri dish with Microban**

Box 2.1 Materials of the future: Light emitting polymers

Most everyday plastics are electrical insulators. In the 1970s the first electrically conducting polymer, poly(ethyne), was produced, and in 1989 the first light-emitting polymers, LEPs, were discovered in Cambridge. Cambridge Display Technology (CDT) is the world leader in this field and has, in partnership with Seiko-Epson, developed a full colour display using LEP technology. LEPs have the advantage over LCD displays that they directly emit light and have a wide viewing angle. Projected future developments include flat screen television and computer displays. For example, in May 2002 CDT signed an agreement with Bayer for using a high resistant version of the polymer, which is called poly(ethene) dioxythiophene poly(phenylethene) sulphonate, PEDOT/PSS. The material is the critical charge transport materials used in LEP display devices that has reduced cross-talk.

CDT is also working with Phillips which is using significant qualities of PolyLED modules, a polymer-based organic light emitting diode display technology. The PolyLED modules consist of a series of emissive polymer-based films, sandwiched between a transparent anode and a metal cathode. Phillips see PolyLED becoming a significant material in display technologies; an example of 'technology-push' innovation.

INTRODUCTION TO PLASTICS

Box 2.3 Relative World Production

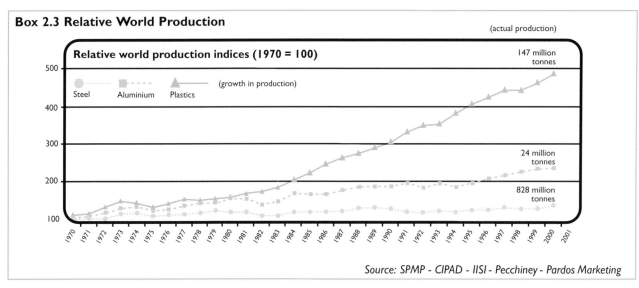

(actual production)

Relative world production indices (1970 = 100)

147 million tonnes

●······· Steel   ■---- Aluminium   ▲—— Plastics   —— (growth in production)

24 million tonnes

828 million tonnes

Source: SPMP - CIPAD - IISI - Pecchiney - Pardos Marketing

2.2 Plastics production

Plastics have been manufactured for several decades. World production of plastics has been rising steadily at about 3.4% each year, and is now in the region of 150 million tonnes. Over the last thirty years the growth in plastics production and use has been higher than for any other material: Box 2.3 shows a comparison between steel, aluminium and plastics.

2.3 Why choose plastics?

Plastics are generally easy to process, thus they can be cost effective, that is high quality products can be manufactured for relatively low costs. Plastics now available include a wide range of properties, some of which are very specialised.

Generally plastics are:

- lightweight
- waterproof
- resistant to atmospheric oxidation

- tough, but, if required, repeated bending can break some
- impermeable to gases
- electrical and /or thermal insulators.

In addition, by varying the additives in plastics, they can be made to be either:

- transparent or opaque
- rigid or flexible.

The specialised properties of plastics are shown in Boxes 2.4 – 2.10.

Box 2.5 Plastics for conducting electricity

In 1971 two Japanese chemists prepared poly(ethyne) which was found to conduct electricity. It was later discovered that the conductivity could be increased significantly by adding small amounts of iodine to the new polymer. Since the discovery of poly(ethyne) a number of other conducting polymers have been prepared. These find a major use in the electronics industry.

Box 2.4 Water soluble plastic

Poly(ethenol) is a plastic which dissolves in water. One use that it is put to is making hospital laundry bags. Soiled laundry is put into the bags. These can then be placed directly into a washing machine where the bag dissolves releasing the dirty washing, thus the workers avoid coming into direct contact with the contaminated laundry.

Flexible 3-inch polyimide foil with a variety of components and electronic test circuits. The circuits still operate when the foil is sharply bent
Photo: Koninklijke Philips Electronics NV

INTRODUCTION TO PLASTICS

Box 2.6 High temperature resistance

Most plastics soften at relatively low temperatures. In the 1960's a team of chemists at ICI developed a new polymer called PEEK (poly ether ether ketone). It has a very high melting point and hence has a high temperature resistance. PEEK is used to make aeroplane engine components and the nose cones of missiles.

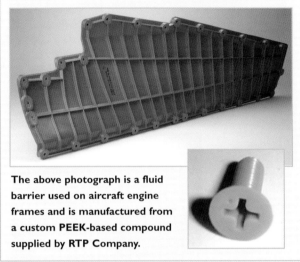

The above photograph is a fluid barrier used on aircraft engine frames and is manufactured from a custom PEEK-based compound supplied by RTP Company.

Box 2.7 Permeability to gases

In 1969, Bob Gore discovered that the plastic poly(tetrafluoroethene), PTFE became porous when stretched. This form of PTFE is called expanded PTFE. The pores are extremely small and will not allow water droplets to pass through but will allow the passage of individual molecules of vapour. A molecule of water is 1/700th of the size of the pores. Thus expanded PTFE is a waterproof 'breathable' fabric. Bob Gore developed a fabric called Gore-tex in which the expanded PTFE is sandwiched between the outer layer of fabric and a layer of another, oil-hating, polymer. This inner polymer layer stops oil and grease from the skin from blocking the pores in the PTFE but allows water vapour to pass through.

Box 2.8 High strength to weight ratio

Kevlar is a material that belongs to the same chemical family as nylon, a polyamide, PA. The differences in their molecular structure are significant resulting in different physical properties. Kevlar fibres are very strong. Kevlar ropes are many times stronger than steel ropes of the same weight. Kevlar has a range of uses including making bullet-proof vests, in aircraft wings and for strengthening tennis racquet frames.

Box 2.9 Piezoelectric (generates electricity when bent or twisted)

Poly(vinylidenefluoride), PVDF is a plastic which is piezoelectric. It can be used in the mouthpiece of telephones – sound waves make it vibrate and this results in the production of a varying electric current. Alternatively if a varying electric current is passed through a piece of this plastic then the plastic vibrates and acts as a loudspeaker.

INTRODUCTION TO PLASTICS

Box 2.10 Biodegradability

A special polyester thread has been produced which is biodegradable. It is used in surgical stitches. Over a period of time the molecules in the thread are broken down (hydrolysed) by water in body fluids into harmless products. The stitches do not need to be removed, they simply dissolve!

Although biodegradable plastics are ideal in some very specific circumstances they are unsuitable for most applications. They use more energy in manufacturing, can degrade in use, and are expensive.

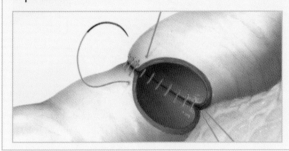

2.4 The relationship of polymers with plastics

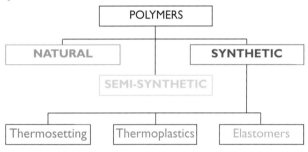

Polymers can be classified as follows:

Early plastics were introduced to replace natural polymers such as horn and ivory (see Boxes 2.11 & 2.12).

Box 2.11 Horn and hoof

Horn and hoof are natural plastic materials, that can be moulded into a variety of shapes. Thin plates could be heated and pressed flat. Some mediaeval buildings had some horn glazing panels in their windows. From the early 17th century it was used for making medallions, and in the 18th century it was moulded into snuff boxes. Previously this had been the province of the hand-carver: the new processing technology enabled cheaper and quicker production. Later still it was pressed to form brooches, in which a high level of detail was possible.

Box 2.12 Parkesine and celluloid

Alexander Parkes, a Birmingham inventor, discovered that he could produce a plastic material by nitrating  cotton with a mixture of concentrated nitric and sulphuric acids. He added various materials as plasticisers, for example camphor, and produced a material called Parkesine. It softened on being heated and could then be shaped.

Parkes' original products were of high quality. But in attempting to drive down production costs, many of his later 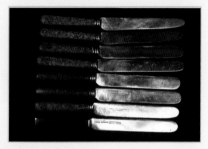 products were prone to warping and cracking, and his company closed down.

Some twenty years later the Hyatt brothers in America were trying to find a substitute for ivory  (an expensive material) in making billiard balls. Based on Parkes' discoveries they used cellulose nitrate, and coined the name 'Celluloid' for the material.

INTRODUCTION TO PLASTICS

Thus, the earliest plastics were natural and semi-synthetic. In the latter case a naturally occurring base material was chemically modified. Box 2.13 gives examples of both natural and semi-synthetic polymers with plastic properties.

Box 2.13 Natural and semi-synthetic polymers

Examples of natural polymers

Amber - fossilised pine resin - is used in jewellery, but rarely for moulded products.

Gutta Percha - made from the sap of the Malayan Palaquim tree - simple to mould, degrades but some examples remain

Horn and hoof - derived from animals - see Box 2.11.

Rubber Latex - made from the resin from rubber trees - is still widely used today but usually in conjunction with other materials

Shellac - made from the secretions of tropical insects

Pitch - widely used for caulking ships, especially when reinforced with straw.

Cellulose - found as cotton or in wood

Tortoiseshell - actually from the Hawksbill turtle - has been widely used for carved objects such as combs, but is not easily mouldable.

Silk - from silk worms

Examples of semi-synthetic polymers

Vuclanite (ebonite) - the first thermosetting plastic to be prepared by chemical modification of a natural material. It was made from latex and sulpur. The Great Exhibition of 1851 had a suite of rooms devoted to displays of objects of the new materials.

Casein (artifical horn) - based on skimmed milk - difficult to mould but frequently carved or turned.

Cellulose acetate - based on cellulose - was also used for a wide variety of products.

Cellulose nitrate - one example is Celluloid (see Box 2.12) which was used for making cine film until as recently as 1952, despite the fact it is highly inflammable. Major uses included hair combs, dressing table ware and toys.

Today the only major use of cellulose nitrate is for table tennis balls.

Other semi-synthetic uses of **cellulose** include packaging (Cellophane) and fibres for textiles (e.g. Rayon and Tricel).

Modern plastics are made up from synthetic or semi-synthetic polymers to which a number of additives (see Chapter 9, section 9.6, p121) have been mixed to modify the physical properties of the polymer.

It is important to appreciate that while all plastics are based upon polymers, it is not true that all polymers are plastic. The synthetic polymer poly(ethene), PE, for example, is a plastic. Cellulose, on the other hand, is a natural polymer but it is not plastic – it cannot be moulded by heat and pressure.

So what is a synthetic polymer?

Polymers ('poly' meaning many and 'mers' meaning parts) are formed when many smaller molecules, monomers, have been chemically bonded together.

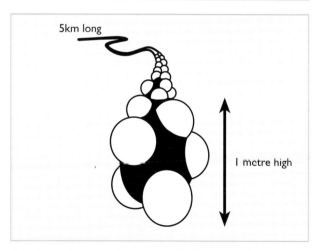

5km long

1 metre high

A typical polymer molecule magnified 50million times

INTRODUCTION TO PLASTICS

Polymerisation is the name given to the process in which monomers react together to form polymer chains. Examples of these processes can be found in Chapter 8.

A polymer can be thought of as being like a chain of paperclips. Each individual paperclip represents a monomer.

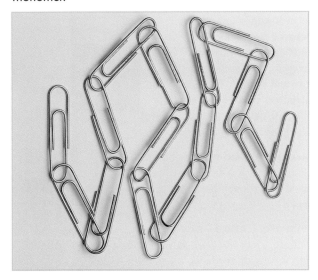

2.5 Synthetic Plastics

Most modern plastics are totally synthetic. The monomers from which they are made are synthesised from carbon compounds that are largely obtained from crude oil. The crude oil is first fractionally distilled and then some of the products are processed further to produce the monomers. Only a small amount (about 4%) of total crude oil production goes into making plastics (see Box 2.14)

Box 2.14 - uses of crude oil

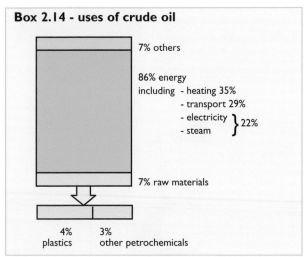

7% others

86% energy
including - heating 35%
         - transport 29%
         - electricity $\}$ 22%
         - steam

7% raw materials

4% plastics   3% other petrochemicals

Synthetic plastics can be divided into two broad groups based on their behaviour when heated:

- Thermoplastics – these soften on being heated and harden again on cooling. They can be shaped while they are soft. Most plastics are thermoplastics.

- Thermosetting plastics - these plastics do not soften when heated (see Chapter 9.5.2); high temperatures simply make the plastic decompose (see Box 2.15).

Box 2.15 Thermosetting plastics

Thermosetting plastics can withstand high temperatures. Bakelite is a common thermosetting plastic which was used to make articles such as radios. It is used to make electrical fittings because it is a very good electrical insulator and can withstand high temperatures if there is a short circuit.

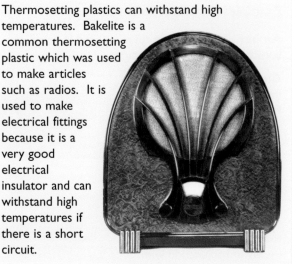

The most common thermoplastics and thermosetting plastics are shown in Box 2.17.

Elastomers are a particular type of thermosetting plastic. (See Chapter 9 for more details). As their name suggests they have elastic or rubber-like properties.

Box 2.16 Thermosoftening plastics

Thermoplastics soften at relatively low temperatures. They are used for applications where high temperature resistance is not important.

INTRODUCTION TO PLASTICS

Box 2.17 Thermoplastics and Thermosetting Plastics

The most common plastics classified according to their response to heat.

Thermoplastics	Thermosetting Plastics
Polyamides e.g. Nylon, PA	Carbamide-methanal
Polycarbonates, PC	Melamine-methanal
Poly(chloroethene), PVC	Phenol-methanal (Bakelite)
Polyesters e.g. PET	Polyurethanes, PU
Poly(ethene), PE	Polyesters unsaturated GRP
Poly(methyl-2-methylpropenoate), PMMA	Epoxy (glue)
Poly(phenylethene), PS	Alkyds (paint)
Poly(propene), PP	
Poly(propenonitrile), PAN	
Poly(tetrafluoroethene), PTFE	

PRODUCTS, BENEFITS AND NEEDS

PRODUCTS, BENEFITS AND NEEDS

3.1 Introduction

The ultimate purpose of all design and technological activity is to improve the quality of life for people. Products are designed to bring 'benefits'. This is as true for plastic products as any other.

The Anywayup Cup (page 41) is a toddler's training cup that does not spill – this improves the quality of life for child and parent alike. TV (page 47) is used to entertain and inform people of all ages. The mobile phone (page 47) brings us the benefits of easy and quick communication, enhancing the quality of human relationships, and safety.

When products are marketed, the emphasis is on the benefits that the product gives to the people who use it. This is often reflected in the advertising – the consumer is offered, for example, status or street credibility, a slim and fit body or the possibility of attractive friends, improved sporting or academic performance, if they buy the product.

This is not to say that designers always get it right. We now realise the widespread use of CFCs in aerosols, fridges and medical products had a detrimental affect on the environment. Some products never take off in the market despite their technical brilliance – the Millennium Dome.

For a product to succeed, it must meet a human need – even if it is need that people did not know they had (see Box 3.1).

Box 3.1 The telephone

When the telephone was invented in 1876, most people had no need for long distance communication. They talked only to people around them. Now in Britain almost every place of work and 95% of all households have a telephone, and over 50% of households of have at least one mobile phone.

Changing lifestyles and work practices both *created* the need for cheap communication at a distance and the demand for the product to make it possible – the telephone. The telephone in turn has had a huge impact on our lifestyles and the way that people work.

The Millennium Dome

PRODUCTS, BENEFITS AND NEEDS

3.2 What are human needs?

As children grow up they learn to distinguish between needs and wants. When a three-year-old says, "I need an ice-cream" the parent might say, "No you don't! You've just had lunch!" Later young people learn to distinguish between physical, intellectual, emotional and social needs, and learn how different products are designed and marketed to meet these needs (see Box 3.2).

Below are examples of plastic products that bring benefits to people through meeting their needs.

Another handle on needs analysis is to distinguish between different levels of need. The social psychologist Maslow talks about a 'hierarchy of needs' (see Box 3.3).

Maslow is suggesting that the lower needs must be satisfied before the higher ones can be addressed.

Some products are designed to meet needs at all these levels (see Box 3.4).

Box 3.3 - Maslow's hierarchy of needs

HIGHEST LEVEL

Need for self - actualisation
(fulfilment, creativity, self-expression)

Esteem needs
(self-respect, self-confidence, prestige)

Belonging and love needs
(needing to be needed)

Safety needs
(free from attack, sheltered from environment)

Physiological needs
(hunger and thirst)

LOWEST LEVEL

Box 3.2 Different types of need

Type of need	Example of need	Product that helps to meet the need	
Physical	To keep dry in the rain	Umbrella (made from polyamide, PA) 	
Intellectual	To stimulate powers of analysis and decision-making	Chess set (made from high density poly(ethene), HDPE or acryonitrile-butadiene-styrene, ABS) 	
Emotional	To engage with the expressive arts	Cinema screen (made from poly(chloroethene), PVC) 	
Social	To party	Hi-fi to produce music (cable is insulated with poly(chloroethene), PVC) 	

PRODUCTS, BENEFITS AND NEEDS

Box 3.4 How new materials and technologies can help to meet our needs - The Bioform bra

All of Maslow's levels are addressed by our need to wear clothes – protection from the elements, comfort and safety, making ourselves attractive to others or enhancing our status, or simply feeling good about ourselves and expressing our personality.

Plastics technology continues to play a major role in the design of clothing. Consider, for example, the needs of the woman with a fuller figure, who wants to look slim and smooth. (This begs the feminist question as to *why* she might want to look like this!). Traditional bra design for the woman with a fuller figure relied on underwire for support. But wires do not follow a natural human form. They are uncomfortable and can produce unsightly bulges. The wire must be covered with fabric, causing ridges. And you cannot machine-wash a garment with wire in it.

Was it possible to rethink the fundamentals of bra design, and to develop a new structure that would enhance bust shape and provide support without sacrificing comfort, especially for the fuller woman?

*The Bioform solution –
a plastics-led innovation*

A multi-disciplinary team of designers, engineers, plastics manufacturers and toolmakers took up the challenge. Together they developed the Bioform bra. The key innovation is the armature, engineered by design to be comfortable and natural in form. This does not look lumpy, does not dig into your back or shoulders, and does not pinch. It provides a contoured three-dimensional support system that is comfortable and good looking. The armature is made from a poly(propene), PP 'keel', with a softer thermoplastic elastomer body-forming support to hold the breast. Poly(propene), PP is tough, non-allergenic and odourless. It can be moulded easily to any shape.

It can go through the washing machine. Lycra (an elastomer) is used for the fabric part of the bra.

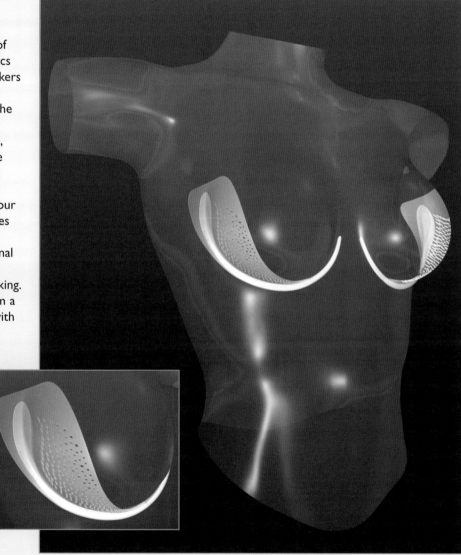

The following four chapters in this book showcase a wide variety of plastic products. In each case they have been developed to address a human need.

Some of our needs develop and change as we move through life. So do the products that bring us benefits through helping to satisfy those needs. In Chapters 4 to 7 we examine how plastics have become beneficial at all stages of life. But first let us showcase four innovatory products. In the first two plastics have an immediate impact in meeting very basic human needs – clean water and shelter. The third and fourth demonstrate how plastics can contribute positively to the environment.

PRODUCTS, BENEFITS AND NEEDS

Show case 1: Water, water everywhere but not a drop to drink

"Water affects every moment of a person's life. It's a basic human need."

Terry Taylor,
Oxfam water engineer

The solution: Cellopore – the Osmotically Driven Self Rehydration Sachet

UCB Films is a global manufacturer of cellulose and other speciality films. The group has a core strategy of innovation based on in-depth research and development, as well as a keen interest in humanitarian causes. UCB Films has been carrying out research into the technologies of cellulose and osmotics since 1995. They came up with the Cellopore concept, and combined these technologies with that of dehydrating foodstuffs.

Cellopore is a self-contained sachet, which converts microbiologically unsafe water to safe water. This can be used for drinking or in conjunction with rehydratable foodstuffs and orally consumed medicines. The Cellopore gives international aid organisations a simple tool to save lives. It works by adapting existing membrane technology, which filters water so effectively that it removes bacteria and viruses. The Cellopore sachet is a simple, self-contained and easy-to-use sachet which enables anyone to produce biologically safe water and food from almost any available water source, even that which is silted or heavily microbiologically contaminated.

When disaster strikes a community, people need clean water – urgently. In a flood, water supplies are contaminated, and the risk of disease easily becomes a very real threat to life. Diarrhoea is the biggest cause of death among children in refugee camps and disaster areas, killing 2.5 million children every year. Unclean water is the major cause. Infected water is responsible for the rapid spread of cholera, typhoid and dysentery, all of which are particularly prevalent in floodwater. The first days of emergencies are often critical, while relief organisations set up the necessary infrastructure.

Emergency organisations need to get safe water through a means that is light, economical to transport, can be installed quickly into a disaster area, and which is easy to use without, if possible, chemicals or fuel.

As it is made from natural cellulose the sachet is biodegradable and easy to open (just tear it) and drink it straight from the sachet, or pour the contents into a clean receptacle. Alternatively, the user can open the

Cellopore in use

PRODUCTS, BENEFITS AND NEEDS

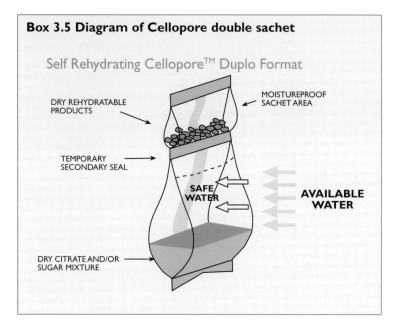

Box 3.5 Diagram of Cellopore double sachet

Self Rehydrating Cellopore™ Duplo Format

DRY REHYDRATABLE PRODUCTS

MOISTUREPROOF SACHET AREA

TEMPORARY SECONDARY SEAL

SAFE WATER

AVAILABLE WATER

DRY CITRATE AND/OR SUGAR MIXTURE

whole top of the sachet and place it in a cup so that only the clean side of the membrane is in contact with the lips.

Sachets are formed from special cellulose film, which acts as a natural nano-filtration membrane. Once placed in the contaminated water, the Cellopore sachet starts to collect safe water by osmosis, excluding more than 99.99% of all known bacteria, viruses and particulate impurities that remain outside of the sachet.

Cellopore comprises mono and duplo sachets. The duplo construction enables a range of products and foodstuffs contained in the upper part of the sachet to be reconstituted inside the sachet. It is simple to use and requires no measuring and no boiling (see Boxes 3.5 and 3.6)

How Cellopore was developed

Professor Michael Wilson (UK) watched a sultana expand, as it absorbed the water through tiny pores in its skin. Inspired by this, he invented the method of purifying water by osmosis using a cellulose membrane. He realised that by combining the technologies of cellulose, osmotics and dehydrated foods, it would be possible to reap enormous benefits for people in disaster areas.

UCB established a team to develop the product, including specialists in cellulose membranes, coating and production engineering. There were advisors, including people from nutritionist networks, humanitarian organisations, supplier and distribution groups, and a number of government aid organisations.

In early experiments the process was found to be too slow – only 200 ml of clean water after 36 hours. Before the product could be considered seriously by the World Health Organisation, this had to be improved.

Further developments led to 500 ml after 6-10 hours.

Before field trials took place, proof was needed that it actually worked. This work was undertaken by the International Centre for Diarrhoeal Disease in Bangladesh, probably the best regarded hospital for water borne diseases in the world. Also, a manufacturing facility that could be licensed by the Medicines Control Agency had to be established. This was achieved with a secondment from another division of UCB (UCB Pharma). Finally, UCB needed to know that the product would be technically and culturally acceptable.

The impact of Cellopore

Early in 2000 UCB decided to go out into the market and actively sell Cellopore. Despite the obvious value of this innovatory product, it was not immediately accepted and brought into widespread use. The route to procurement was more complicated than anticipated. Approval time for aid budgets was under-estimated. There was unexpected bureaucracy surrounding risk-averse governments and relief organisations. Although the original sachet was completed in1999, Cellopore was, in 2002, undergoing tests and being evaluated. Small-scale trials have been successful in Mozambique, the Philippines, Bangladesh and India. They are at the stage of proceeding on large-scale evaluation in a real situation in collaboration with the major world aid organisations to finalise this long evaluation process.

Box 3.6 Benefits of Cellopore

- Clean safe water from almost any available water source

- Simple to use

- Excludes more than 99.99% of micro-organisms - cysts, bacteria and viruses

- No chemical purification required

- Unaffected by silted water

- Totally self-contained

- Hygienic delivery system

- Does not require fuel

- A wide range of products from drinking water to foodstuffs and oral medicines can be used. Assures correct composition with no need for measuring

- Easy to transport, dry, lightweight and compact

- Biodegradable/compostable

PRODUCTS, BENEFITS AND NEEDS

Show case 2: Shelters in emergencies

Many countries in the world are prone to natural disasters.

When an earthquake, hurricane or flood strikes a community and many people are made homeless, there is a need for emergency shelter that is:

- easy to transport – ideally flat-packed and lightweight

- easy to erect without any tools

- without poles or frames

- water repellent and moisture free

- easy to keep clean

- able to offer disaster victims some privacy and dignity.

The design story: the Board-a-Line Emergency Shelter

While working on search-and-rescue missions in Rwanda, engineer Nigel Borrell noticed how sometimes the efforts of relief agencies to provide shelter often had a bad impact on the environment, as trees were cut to make wooden supports. Was it possible to develop a shelter that was lightweight, simple to erect, self-standing and recyclable?

The origins of the emergency shelter actually came from thinking about a hospital bed. Nigel saw patients being treated on tarmac and began to think about a cheap, portable bed that could be sterilised. When looking for materials for the bed, he came across twin-wall fluted poly(propene), PP, which was available in different thicknesses and strengths and could be folded. It was already known for its thermal insulation properties – for example it is widely used for keeping fish cold in ice.

A further strand to the thinking was flat-pack furniture, which can be assembled by slotting components together. Putting these together in a new context the idea of the *Board-a-Line shelter* was born.

Nigel teamed up with Steve Gosney (expertise in poly(propene), PP technology) Lara Sullivan (marketing and public relations) and Tonya Crew (commercial administration) to form PP Global Technology, a very new British design and manufacturing company that supplies a range of poly(propene) PP products for people who are displaced by a disaster. One of their first products was the Board-a-Line Emergency Shelter.

The materials

The shelter is made from twin-wall, fluted poly(propene), PP, which is made through extrusion (see

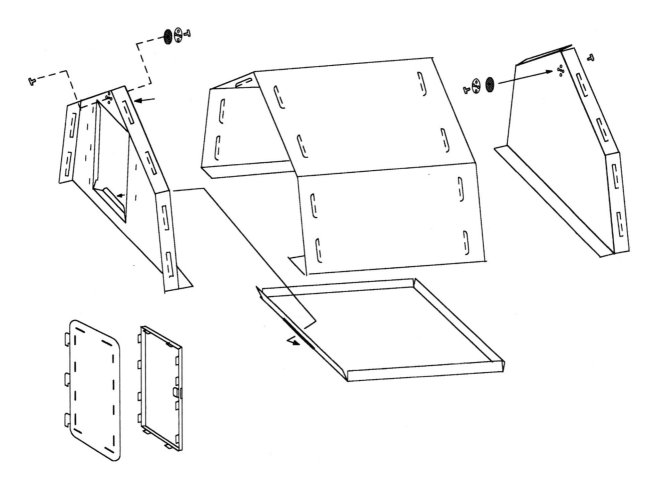

PRODUCTS, BENEFITS AND NEEDS

Chapter 8). It has six main components: the sides and roof are from a single sheet that is scored so that it can be folded easily. The two ends slot into place and hold the whole structure rigid. The floor comes as a separate component, and the door is formed from two components. The shelter can be assembled quickly on any ground surface. It is water repellent and moisture free. The insulated units provide greater protection than traditional tents or plastic sheeting. The lightest version weighs only 14 kg. They are flat-packed for ease of transportation and storage, and can be stockpiled without risk of deterioration. The surface is washable, includes a fire retardant, and can include anti-bacterial, non-toxic repellents to diminish the risk of spreading disease. Anti-bacterial properties are achieved through spraying the panels: the treatment lasts about 6 months. Fire retardant properties are achieved through an additive being included when the poly(propene), PP is made. As poly(propene), PP can be bent many times without causing fatigue, the shelter can be assembled and taken down many times. Thus the shelter meets all the requirements listed above.

The Board-a-Line Emergency Shelter has won the status of a Millennium Product. PP Global Technology is committed to design and manufacture and supply a full range of emergency relief supplies, using advanced PP technology. Products in development include a hospital or school shelter, a hospital bed, a baby incubator, a boat, shower blocks and latrines, and an irrigation/water system.

PRODUCTS, BENEFITS AND NEEDS

Show case 3: The Eden Project – an example of ground breaking design made possible by new plastics

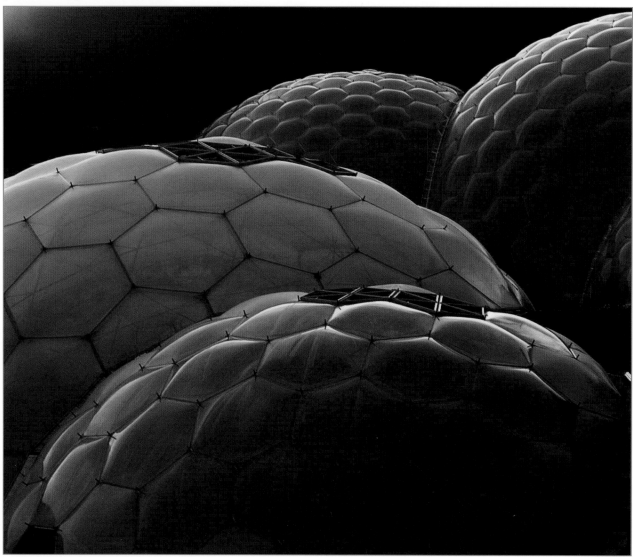

The sun sets over the giant biomes of the Eden Project near St. Austell, Cornwall

The Eden Project in an old Cornish quarry is the largest greenhouse in the world – a showcase for global bio-diversity and human dependence on plants. There are climate-controlled biomes, a biomes link building and a Visitors' Centre. The biomes encapsulate the humid tropics and warm temperate regions. The surrounding landscape represents a cool temperate zone.

The challenge

The complex had to reflect the environmental theme of the project. The structure had to be built from components that could be transported and assembled easily. It had to be very light and strong, and able to withstand large pressures from the wind. The transparent units had to allow natural light to pass through (glass allows 90% of the light spectrum), and

not be affected by ultra-violet light. Above all, an organic form was needed that was an integral part of the whole composition, which mirrors the highly contoured Cornish landscape.

The solution

The Nicholas Grimshaw partnership developed a series of spheres of differing diameters which suited the site and the internal spatial requirements, such as the waterfalls which cascade down the quarry walls. The biomes are a series of inter-linked geodesic domes, with a minimal surface area providing the maximum enclosed volume. The hexagonal structure allows for variations in the topography of the quarry, removing the need for extensive rock blasting.

PRODUCTS, BENEFITS AND NEEDS

Box 3.7 Ethyltetrafluoroethylene, ETFE

The characteristics of ETFE

- It is far lighter than glass.

- It has low embodied energy (the energy required to manufacture it).

- It has a very long life expectancy.

- It is completely recyclable.

- 98% of the light spectrum passes through it.

- When it deforms due to wind pressure, the yield to strength ratio remains the same (glass would shatter).

The materials

The frame is made from steel, consisting of tubular compressive members and standard cast connectors. The glazing panels are made from triple-layered, inflated, transparent ethyltetrafluoroethylene (ETFE) foil pillows (see Box 3.7). The ETFE was extruded into a continuous roll 1 500 mm wide, and then heat welded to get the required width. The design for finishing the edges was taken from ship technology: essentially it is the same as for a sail.

Success

The popularity of the project has exceeded everyone's expectations, not least because of people's fascination with gardens, plants and the environment, and the awe inspiring, otherworldly appearance of the biomes.

PRODUCTS, BENEFITS AND NEEDS

Show case 4: The 100% degradable polythene sack

The challenge

Currently the UK has to dispose of 120 million tonnes of total waste each year, which includes a million tonnes of plastic. Each British household throws away over a tonne of waste each year. Much is in plastic bin-liners, that have to be strong, tough and tear-resistant. The trouble is that most bin-liners are not bio-degradable.

Traditionally the 'solution' has been to bury waste and bin-liners in landfill sites. But some of this plastic resurfaces as an environmental hazard, either through littering the countryside, or getting into the food chain. What is needed is a bin-liner that decomposes totally, without damaging the environment – and which would conform to the legal requirements of the European Union (see Box 3.8).

The solution

Symphony Environmental Ltd, a British company, claim to have developed a totally degradable poly(ethene), PE sack, the Tuffy SPI-TEK. Currently they are manufacturing refuse sacks, swing bin liners, pedal bin liners, food freezer bags, dog waste sacks, and they are investigating other applications for this environmentally friendly solution. As the polythene sack breaks down, it leaves behind only carbon dioxide and water. The plastic degrades in as little as 60 days, or as long as 5-6 years, depending on the requirements of the product. This is known as Degradable Compostable Plastics technology, DCP for short.

How it works

Essentially, the degradation is a two-part process.

DCP technology uses an additive which is combined with a blend of poly(ethene), PE, resins during the production process. The manufacturers claim that the environmental impact of the additive is negligible, and the finished product retains all the dynamic qualities of standard polythene. The product is engineered to maintain its stability and integrity for its calculated cycle of usage.

The degradation process, which can be controlled, commences with any combination of heat, light and stress. Once initiated it will continue even in a landfill or under water. As the polymer molecules are broken up, the small fragments produced in the presence of air are converted to carbon dioxide and water. The intermediate degradation products (the precursors to CO_2 and water) are still polymeric. The degrading material still contains large, water insoluble molecules, but no acidic or alkaline soluble fragments that can contaminate the leachate or water table.

Eventually, the resins' molecules will become short enough to be assimilated by micro-organisms (after the fragments become water wettable but before they become water soluble). The resulting end product is minute quantities of carbon dioxide and water, exactly the same products that we exhale when we breathe.

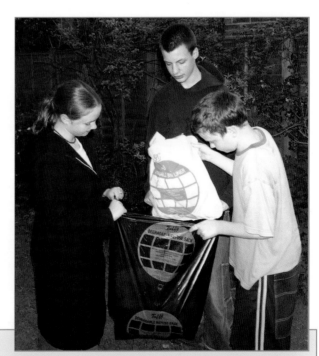

Packaging (Essential Requirements) Regulations 1998 (S.I. 1998 No 1165)

The Producer Responsibility Obligations (Packaging Waste) Regulations 1997 stipulates that at least 50% by weight of all packaging waste should be recovered, and that 25% should be recycled, with a minimum of 15% for each material. In the past, designers sought to minimise the amount of packaging to reduce production costs and, of course, for environmental reasons. Now producers will pay a penalty if they fail to meet targets: this can lead to higher costs and subsequent loss of market competitiveness.

Box 3.8 The effect of legal requirements

The European Union requires that:

- packaging must be minimal and subject to safety and hygiene, whilst being acceptable to the consumer;

- noxious or hazardous substances in packaging must be minimised in emissions, ash or leachate from incineration or landfill;

- packaging must be recoverable through at least one of the following: material recycling, incineration with energy recovery and composting or biodegradation;

- packaging maybe reusable.

THE VERY YOUNG

THE VERY YOUNG

All young children need food, warmth and protection from the environment, and love. A premature baby needs a higher level of protection and monitoring.

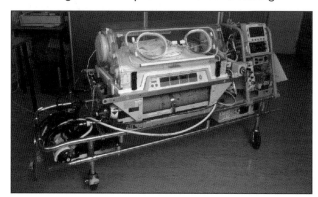

The casing of the incubator is made from poly(methyl 2-methyl propenoate), PMMA, or polycarbonate, PC. These are tough and transparent, and easy to keep clean. The tubes are made from poly(chloroethene), PVC.

4.1 Monitoring a small child

Once a child is in bed, parents need to listen for crying or coughing. The electronics of this baby monitor are housed in a casing made from acrylonitrile-butadiene-styrene, ABS.

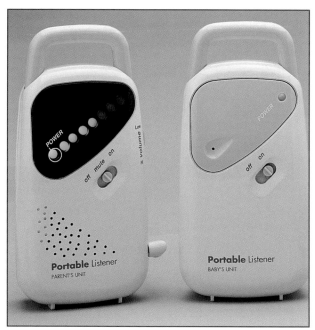

Baby monitor

4.2 Transporting a small child

Parents also need to transport the baby, who in turn needs to be comfortable and protected from the elements.

This Mothercare three-wheel buggy uses a variety of different plastics. The manufacturers, Petite Star,

The Mothercare Urban twin three wheeler

describe buggy design as a high-tec business, not unlike Formula 1 racing! They aim to achieve the optimum compromise between strength, lightness, looks, feel and costs. The buggy must be user friendly *and* aesthetically pleasing. To achieve this most buggies have numerous plastic components, some of which might be made from metal encased in plastic, or one plastic inside another, so that the grip has a rubberised feel for example. Materials are chosen with regard to the stresses and strains and the climatic conditions in which the product will be used. New materials and compounds open up new design possibilities – buggy development never stands still.

4.3 Feeding a baby

The need

Sooner or later, nearly all babies are fed from a bottle (see Box 4.1). Some mothers choose this option from the start, but other mothers switch to using a bottle when they go back to work. A common practice is for the mother to breastfeed her baby in the morning and evening, and to express her milk and store it in bottles so that another carer can feed the baby with the mother's milk during the day. To do this the mother will use a breast pump (see Box 4.2). Breast pumps can also be used if the breasts are engorged (painful and swollen), to ease the discomfort between feeds, and to help the baby latch on to the breast.

THE VERY YOUNG

Box 4.1 Bottle feeding

Colic is a catch-all term used to describe prolonged crying, fussing and discomfort. It is often caused by the baby taking air into the stomach whilst feeding. Air intake and colic is less likely to occur if the baby is suckling. Suckling is a long, slow, continuous lip type of suck, involving the nipple and areola when the tongue moves from front to back In contrast, sucking is a short, fast action involving the lips only on the surface of the nipple. A child is more likely to suckle from a bottle if it mimics the form and function of the breast.

The design challenge

The design challenge is to have a feeding bottle that allows the baby to suckle continuously, reducing the risk of swallowing air. The bottle also needs to be easy to hold, filled and cleaned (sterilised) easily, and leak-proof. It also has to be at a cost that people find reasonable.

Most feeding bottles and sterilising equipment are made from plastics - the bottle in the picture is silicone, acrylonitrile-butadiene-styrene, ABS, poly(propene), PP, and polycarbonate, PC. The use of plastics allows bottles to be sterilised easily and shaped in a way that is natural for the baby and easy to use.

The AVENT solution: The Anti-colic bottle

The AVENT silicone teats are made from soft medical grade silicone and shaped to mimic the breast in form and function. Some teats have a slot instead of a hole: turning the bottle controls the rate of flow.

The bottle is easy to clean, to hold and is leak-proof.

The materials

The *teat* is formed from liquid silicone rubber (50/50) – to make it feel right in the baby's mouth.

The *bottle* is made from polycarbonate, PC. This is clear, tough, hard and does not scratch easily. Although acrylonitrile-butadiene-styrene, ABS, would have given a shinier finish and greater depth of gloss, this would not have been suitable for boiling.

The *screw-on fitting* is from poly(propene), PP.

The *lid* is also from poly(propene), PP, but of a different grade. It is a random co-polymer, selected for its clarity. Pigment is added to make it slightly coloured whilst retaining its transparent properties.

Methods of processing

The *teat* is injection moulded. As it is a thermosetting plastic, the barrel of the moulding machine must be cool. The two-part mixture is injected into the tool, which is then heated. The teat cures in less than a minute, after which is can be ejected. The *bottle* is also injection stretch blow **moulded**. But as it is a thermoplastic, the barrel is hot and the tool cool. If it was simply blow moulded, the ridges of the screw would appear inside the bottle, making it hard to clean.

Injection blow moulding involves a two part process. The parison (unmoulded plastic) is injection moulded to form the neck detail only, which leaves the inside smooth and the thread very precise. The remainder of the parison is then blow moulded to form the body of the body. Injection stretch blow moulding adds another feature: the body part of the parison is stretched before being blow moulded, which aligns the molecules leading to less stress in the moulding and better clarity. The *screw-on fitting* and *lid* are also injection moulded. For more detail on manufacturing processes see Chapter 8.

Avent Silicone Teat.

Patented skirt collapses to let air into bottle as baby sucks. Prevents vacuum build up. Pliable, human shaped, ribbed nipple never collapses.

THE VERY YOUNG

Box 4.2 The Avent Isis breast pump

There is strong evidence that babies do best if they have nothing but breast milk for the first four to six months of life. This may be important if there is any diabetes or allergies in the family as the use of formula milk increases the risk of diabetes, asthma or eczema. Many working mothers therefore prefer to provide their baby with their own milk rather than formula milk.

Breast pump technology has been around in hospitals for many years, based on the electric milking machines used by the dairy industry. Older pumps use force and suction to extract the milk – a noisy and uncomfortable process. Now breast pumps have been developed that reproduced the natural suckling of a baby, and are more gentle, quiet and discreet.

The key feature of the Isis breast pump is the silicone petal massager (a), which fits naturally onto the breast. As the pump is operated using the handle (d), the petals flex in and out, gently massaging the nipple and areola and stimulating the 'let down' reflex, painlessly and naturally. The suction of the diaphragm (c) is controlled just through fingertip pressure.

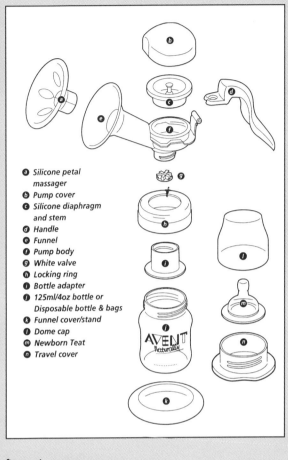

- **a** Silicone petal massager
- **b** Pump cover
- **c** Silicone diaphragm and stem
- **d** Handle
- **e** Funnel
- **f** Pump body
- **g** White valve
- **h** Locking ring
- **i** Bottle adapter
- **j** 125ml/4oz bottle or Disposable bottle & bags
- **k** Funnel cover/stand
- **l** Dome cap
- **m** Newborn Teat
- **n** Travel cover

A second challenge is to produce a bottle which mimics breast feeding as closely as possible. This is to reduce colic, and if a child has become used to breast feeding, to facilitate the switch to the bottle.

4.4 Drinks for the older child

The need

Mandy Haberman, an established inventor of products for very young children, was visiting a friend when she noticed the friend's child was spraying everything with blackcurrant juice from a training cup. This is a problem shared by many parents.

Children drinking from training cups like to wave them, bang them and generally have fun. The result can be very messy. An additional problem arises if the child is being taken out. A drink for the child will be needed, but traditional training cups leak. Mandy Haberman set out to design a cup that automatically sealed when it came out of the child's mouth so that it would not spill, even if it was shaken or dropped, a training cup that was easy to use, easy to clean and was virtually indestructible.

The Anywayup Cup

THE VERY YOUNG

The Haberman solution – the Anywayup Cup

The Anywayup Cup is an innovative, toddlers' training cup incorporating a patented, unique valve that only allows liquid through when the child sucks the spout, ensuring no more spills. The product works because the lid on the Cup forms an air-tight seal with the base. When the child sucks on the spout the simple slit-valve distorts upwards, releasing the liquid, but when the child stops sucking, the air rushing back in pulls the valve back down to shut perfectly every time (see Box 4.3).

Box 4.3 How the Anywayup cup valve works

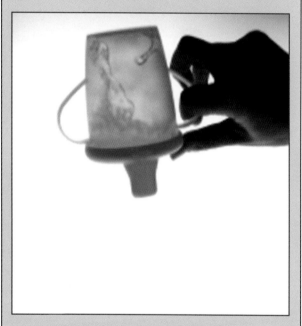

The valve is formed from a simple membrane, moulded directly under the hole in the spout. It is a simple, slit-valve, domed against the direction of flow. As the child sucks, the dome distorts upwards, opening the valve. As liquid is withdrawn, negative pressure builds up inside the cup, but this is almost totally relieved as air is drawn back into the cup between sucks. When the child stops drinking, a slight negative pressure remains inside. When

 removed from the child's mouth, atmospheric pressure and the inherent resilience of the valve material ensure that the valve returns to its tightly shut, default position. The shape of the valve and the residual negative pressure prevent the valve from opening until the child sucks again, even if the cup is turned upside down and vigorously shaken.

The materials

The base is made from poly(propene), PP, and the lid from high density poly(ethene), HDPE. Initially they tried a PP lid, but it was too rigid for this particular design. The fit of lid to base is critical, as the rim must be leak-proof – HDPE is slightly more yielding and dissimilar materials form a better seal. The valve is made from Evoprene, which is a thermoplastic elastomer, based on PP. It is soft, almost rubbery. The only additives used are pigments for colouring and pearlised finish, which account for 1 – 2% by weight.

Method of manufacture

The base and lid are injection moulded. The Evoprene valve is insert-moulded: the formed lid is placed in a second mould, into which is placed about 2 gm of Evoprene. This is formed into a slight concave dome. The valve sticks in place because of the similar molecular structure. A slitting machine then cuts a slit to complete the process.

The development of a successful product

Mandy Haberman invented the Anywayup Cup in 1990. Having developed the prototype and patented the idea, she tried to interest companies in manufacturing it under license – without success. So she established her own company to produce it, she teamed up with V&A Marketing as sales agents. Eventually, she licensed the manufacturing to V&A, which now sells over five million cups a year. She also has an American licensee and between the two, over 10 million cups are now sold worldwide, each year.

Mandy Haberman, Inventor of the Year 1990

THE VERY YOUNG

Children's toys

Children's toys need to be non-toxic, strong and easy to clean.

Most children in Britain will have come across Duplo and Lego. They are a superbly flexible 'toys' which allow children to develop hand-eye co-ordination and fine motor skills, encourage their creativity, planning and experimentation, and give hours of fun. When they are a bit older children might build up a collection of Lego Technic, which makes possible more complicated constructions with moving parts, gears and possibly electric motors. One of the characteristics of Duplo and Lego components is their precision manufacture (they are injection moulded to a tolerance of ± 0.005 mm). This means that the parts will always join together.

The basic Lego or Duplo brick is made from acrylonitrile-butadiene-styrene, ABS. The most obvious benefits derived from using this material are the bright, shiny colours that can be achieved, as well as its ability to maintain its shape and its resistance to scratching. ABS is also non-toxic, resistant to perspiration, saliva and other substances with which Lego elements often come into contact. The transparent elements in Lego are made from polycarbonate, PC. Lego can be bought in buckets that can also be used for storing the bricks: these buckets are made from poly(propene), PP. Lego kits usually come in some sort of plastics packaging. Polyethylene terephthalate, PET or styrenebutadiene, SB is used for vacuum-formed packaging components, PP as film for outer wrappings, PET as window film, and poly(ethene), PE as shrink-wrapped film.

Children love Lego

Play equipment

As children get mobile they need plenty of exercise to develop healthily. Parents need equipment that is strong and easy to clean, and which will be attractive to the children. This slide is made from high density poly(ethylene), HDPE components, which have been made through injection moulding.

Soft toys

For the child who likes softer toys, plastics are also useful. Beanie Babies® are made from polyester cover material with bagged poly(ethene), PE, pellets inside. These appeal as much to many older children as to the very young!

Beanies appeal to children of all ages

YOUNG PEOPLE

YOUNG PEOPLE

As children grow, they become more aware of other people, and the world around them. They still have the basic needs of food and water, shelter and love.

They develop new needs to keep in touch with parents and friends – many now have their own mobile phones.

5.1 The mobile phone

Mobile phones are approximately 50% plastic: their durability and flexibility are essential for their low cost, low weight and modern designs. The case needs to:

- have high colour stability and impact performance

- be resistant to ultra violet light

- be easy to form and to recycle.

Typically they are made from polycarbonate, PC. The display window or lens is a critical part of any mobile phone. This is especially so as mobile phones are becoming increasingly screen centred, as users seek Internet connectivity in smaller and lighter products. The display window must have high clarity as well as be resistant to scratching and impact. Both PC and acrylic have been used. Many windows now have a PC film,

back-moulded onto a firmer PC resin. The printed circuit board might be made from epoxy and polyphenylene oxide, PPO resins, chosen for their thermal and electrical properties, and because they are easy to process. The casing for the charger could be made from polybutylene terephthalate, PBT (very good electrical properties, chemical resistance, high temperature performance, flame retardance and fast moulding), or from polyphenylene ether-polyamide resin, PPE-PA, which is paintable, is good in low as well as high temperatures and resistant to chemicals.

Television and music

Most children like to listen to music. They might have a hi-fi in their bedroom, or a personal stereo. They use television for entertainment, and to learn more about the world outside the home.

At present most CDs and DVDs are made from polycarbonate, PC. But soon more will be made from poly(methyl methacrylate), PMMA, as it is more scratch resistant, and the resin costs less. The hi-fi casing might be made from acrylonitrile-butadiene-styrene, ABS (thermal stability, impact resistance, good surface quality, wide range of colours, ease of moulding) or a polycarbonate/acrylonitrile-butadiene-styrene, PC/ABS alloy which will have greater UV stability. The speakers could be made from polybutylene terephthalate, PBT, which is dense but easy to process, and has useful noise attenuation characteristics.

A TV housing is likely to be made from acrylonitrile-butadiene-styrene, ABS or polycarbonate/acrylonitrile-butadiene-styrene, PC/ABS. The chassis and backplate are more likely to made from polyphenylene oxide, PPO because of its electrical properties, high temperature performance and flame resistance.

DVD technology is revolutionising home entertainment

YOUNG PEOPLE

5.2 Transport

Many children and teenagers get around on bicycles. Although the frames are metal, many of the smaller components are made from plastics – seats, cable housings, brake blocks, lights and tyres.

5.3 Clothes

As children grow older, they feel the need to look good as well as feel comfortable. They become more fashion-conscious. Most fabrics are constructed from yarns which, in turn, are made from fibres.

Many modern clothes are based on polymers

Box 5.1 Sources of fibres used in textiles

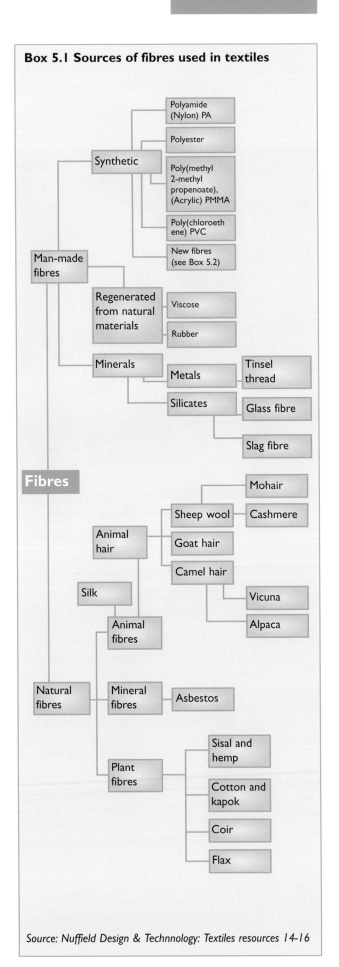

Source: Nuffield Design & Technnology: Textiles resources 14-16

YOUNG PEOPLE

Box 5.2 New fibres and fabrics

New fabrics are constantly being developed. This offers exciting new design opportunities.

Date	Innovation	Key features	Applications
1910	Rayon	The first artificial fibre, made from cellulose (wood pulp). Soft, comfortable, highly absorbent, dyes and prints well. But some rayon textiles can shrink and need dry cleaning.	Clothes – blouses, dresses, jackets, lingerie, linings, millinery, trousers, sports shirts, suits, ties, work clothes Household – bedspreads, blankets, curtains, sheets, table cloths, upholstery
1924	Acetate	Cellulose based (wood pulp or cotton). Luxurious appearance, can be crisp or soft, takes colour extremely well, very soft and drapeable. Shrink resistant, low absorbency, no pilling.	Clothes – blouses, dresses, linings, special occasion apparel Household – upholstery, curtains, bedspreads
1938	Teflon	Withstands temperatures from −240°C to + 260°C, highly inert, low coefficient of friction. Originally used for non-stick pots and pans (1950s).	Protective coatings for fabrics (from 1960s) Stain-proof fabrics (from 1990s)
1939	Nylon Polyamide(PA)	Light, exceptionally strong, good drapeability, abrasion-resistant, easy to wash, resistant to shrinking and wrinkling, low absorbency, fast drying, can be precoloured or dyed, resistant to damage by oil and many chemicals. But has poor resistance to prolonged exposure to sun.	Clothes – swimwear, active wear, sports wear, underclothes, foundation garments, trousers, jackets, raincoats, windbreakers Household – carpets, rugs, curtains, upholstery, bedspreads Other – luggage, back-packs, life-vests, umbrellas, sleeping bags, tents
1941	Polyester	The most widely used manufactured fibre. Strong, crisp or soft, does not stretch or shrink, can be washed or dry cleaned, dries quickly, resilient with excellent pleat retention, resistant to wrinkles, abrasion and most chemicals. But problems with stain removal, static and pilling.	Clothing – almost everything Household – curtains, floor coverings fibre fill, upholstery, bedding, soft toys
1950	Acrylic (poly(methyl 2-methyl propenoate) PMMA)	A soft, drapeable fabric, warm without being heavy. Takes colour beautifully. Flexible aesthetics – can be wool-like or have cotton feel. Resilient, retaining shape and pleats well. Resists shrinkage, wrinkling, moths, oil, chemicals and sunlight degradation. Easy to wash and dry. Possible problems with static and pilling.	Clothes – sweaters, socks, fleeces, circular knitted clothes, sportswear Home – blankets, throws, upholstery, awnings, outdoor furniture, rugs, floor coverings
1959	Spandex (best known through DuPont's brand name – Lycra®)	Originally developed as a substitute for rubber. Light, exceptional elasticity (can be stretched over 500% without breaking), abrasion resistant, soft, smooth and supple, resistant to body oils, perspiration, lotions, detergents.	Used with other fibres to provide contour-hugging fabric – especially athletic wear, swimwear, foundation garments, ski clothes, trousers, hosiery, socks, belts. Sometimes replaced by elastoester which has polyester-like qualities

YOUNG PEOPLE

Box 5.2 Fibres and fabrics cont...			
Date	**Innovation**	**Key features**	**Applications**
1961 (1970)	Spunbonded olefin and poly(propene), PP, also called polyolefin	The lightest and least absorbent of all manufactured fibres. Strong, abrasion resistant, resistant to stain, static, sunlight, odour, chemicals, mildew, perspiration, rot and weather. Fast drying, colourfast.	Clothes – active wear (e.g. for back-packing, canoeing, mountain climbing), sportswear, jeans, socks, underwear, linings Household – indoor and outdoor carpets, carpet backing, upholstery, wall coverings, furniture and bedding construction fabrics
1972	Kevlar®	Exceptionally strong, light and stiff makes it suitable for specialist clothing.	Clothes – astronauts' suits, bullet-proof vests
1976	Gore-tex	Waterproof semi-permeable fabric that allows water vapour to pass from wearer to outside.	Outdoor clothing, protective clothing for astronauts and pilots, surgeons' gowns
1989	Microfibres	Ultra fine fibres (less that 1/100th of human hair in thickness) can be made from acrylic, nylon, polyester and rayon, giving exceptional drape and surface texture – they are very soft, with a luxurious and silken suede touch. Can be washed or dry cleaned, do not shrink, retain pleats, and insulate well against wind, rain and cold.	Clothes – luxury blouses, dresses, separates. Sportswear, ties, scarves, underwear, hosiery, outerwear, rainwear. Household – curtains, upholstery, sheets, towels, blankets
1993	Lyocell (best known through Tencel® brand)	The newest cellulose-based fibre. Similar to rayon in appearance, but much stronger when wet and more durable. Washable, soft, excellent drape, absorbent, takes dyes and prints well. Environmentally friendly, lyocell is produced from the wood pulp of trees grown specifically for this purpose. It is specially processed, using a solvent spinning technique in which the dissolving agent is recycled, reducing environmental effluents.	Clothes – dresses, suits, sportswear, trousers, jackets, blouses, skirts. Household – curtains, upholstery, bedspreads, table linens, sheets, tea towels, bath towels
1997	Polylactic acid (PLA)	A fibre made from a corn-based polymer that comes from renewable sources and is biodegradable like natural fibres. Similar to cotton in appearance, and breathes well. Excellent drapeability, and resistant to flames and UV light.	Clothes – lingerie, men's shirts, active sportswear, outerwear

Sources: Nuffield Design & Technology: Textiles   DuPont web site   The Fabric University web site

YOUNG PEOPLE

Box 5.3 Tactel

Tactel is a nylon fibre, made by DuPont. It is widely used in a wide variety of clothing products – from lingerie to sportswear and evening wear.

It can be woven, knitted or moulded. It is resistant to abrasion and tear, and is easy to wash. It comes in more than a dozen forms, each engineered for specific properties such as metallic shine (Tactel Metallics), multicolours in a single yarn (Tactel Prisma), allowing moisture to be drawn from the skin and to evaporate (Tactel Aquator), and many others. It comes in different cross sections and thickness, which allow for variation in texture, lustre, drape. Altogether, it is a thoroughly modern fibre, which allows designers a huge range of creative possibility.

For a full exploration of this material, see http://www.dupont.com/tactel/index.html

Increasing we are using fibres based on polymers, in particular polyamides, PA - often called nylon, polyester, poly(methyl 2-methyl propenoate), PMMA - often called acrylic, poly(chloroethene), PVC, viscose and rubber. These are chosen for their aesthetic appeal, hard wearing or crease-proof properties, ease of washing, and resistance to wear and tear. There are two groups of natural polymers viscose and rubber. One of the attractions of viscose is the feel against the skin and moisture absorbing properties. Rubber, an elastomer, is the base of Lycra which stretches to fit the body, and is widely used in tight, fashionable clothes and sportswear. Box 5.1 shows the place of polymer based fibres – these are shown in bold type.

5.4 Recreation for young people

Sports manufacturers are increasingly using plastics, where the materials have to meet exacting requirements for mechanical strength and weight to performance ratio.

For some applications several plastics may have properties which make them suitable for making the object. Some plastics are more expensive than others. Also, methods of construction affect the cost. In applications like these the choice of material will determine whether the product will be top of the range or a cheaper brand.

Poly(propene), PP, and polyurethanes, (PU), are used in ski boot shells (see Box 5.4) as they give rigidity, and resistance to impact, cold and water.

Ski undersides are made from high density poly(ethene), HDPE, with a very high molecular weight*, which combines a smooth gliding surface with good abrasion resistance.

Expanded poly(phenylethane), EPS or polyurethane, EPU, foams are very light: as a result, sailboards weigh a mere 8 to 12 kg for a length of 2 to 3.5 m and are, of course, unsinkable. Poly(urethane), EPU foams can also be either highly rigid or very flexible. Rigid foams make up ski cores, whereas flexible easy-to-mould foams are used to make the base of ski boot linings, for which their very good insulating properties are a bonus.

The vast range of polyurethane, PU foams is very much in demand for athletic tracks and sports grounds, although poly(chloroethene) PVC can also be used in this application. Sports surfaces made from plastics greatly reduce energy loss due to friction and to foot/ground impact. Furthermore, they are durable and withstand the effects of adverse weather: athletes no longer have to run on 'cinder' tracks.

* HDPE containing on average, very long molecules of poly(ethene).

YOUNG PEOPLE

Box 5.4 Ski boots

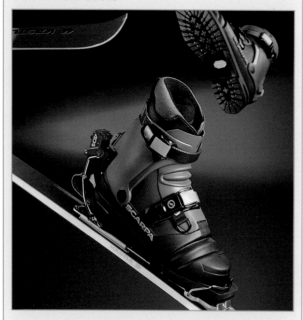

Ski boots used to be made of five or six layers of leather, and consequently were very heavy, not entirely impermeable to water, difficult to keep in good condition, and very expensive to make.

The main components of today's boots are in the lining (polyurethane, PU, foam) and in the shell (poly(propene), PP, poly(urethanes), PU, or polyamides, PA), all of which are lightweight, waterproof, easy to keep clean and inexpensive.

As for sports shoes, plastics such as polyether-block-amide, PEBA, offer benefits of rigidity and elasticity, and the capacity to recover their original shape, even after severe deformation. PEBA is used extensively in the

soles of football boots and long distance ski boots, torsion bars of tennis shoes, and soles and spikes of athletic shoes.

Textile fibres made from plastics such as polyethylene terephthalate, PET, are of value to athletes. Clothing featuring synthetic fibres have many benefits: light weight and durable, not to mention the qualities of a second skin; polyamide, PA, polyether-block-amide, PEBA, and poly(tetrafluoroethene), PTFE, for example, can be woven into 'breathable' fabrics, which let perspiration through but act as a barrier to rain. These products are used for clothing, tents, rucksacks and sleeping bags.

Polyamides, PA, are not just used in fibre form. For example, the polyamide, nylon 11 is injection moulded into components such as the shells of competition ski boots. Similarly, ski fastenings, which were previously made of metal, are now made from glass fibre reinforced polyamide, or from polyacetal, POM. This offers improved lateral flexibility, as well as increased release safety in the event of a fall. These materials are self-lubricating, even at -20°C, a characteristic which metals lack. They remain reliable and effective for years, and require no particular maintenance (see Box 5.4).

Tennis racket with Kevlar® in the frame and nylon strings.

Box 5.5 Kevlar® in sports equipment

Kevlar®: tougher than steel

Kevlar® is a polyaramid fibre which is also widely used in sport. It is so tough that it is used in preference to steel for cables used for mooring boats.

Kevlar® is both flexible and extremely strong. It is used in combination with polyamides, PA, to coat ski cores with a strong shell. Light and effective in traction, it can absorb impact and vibrations, and imparts more rigidity to skis.

Kevlar® is also used in golf club handles. The good torsional strength means it is tough and accurate. This, together with its light weight, means that club heads can be made heavier so they can strike the ball even further.

In tennis racket frames the use of Kevlar® reduces the impact from the ball. Bonded with carbon fibre within epoxy resins it offers outstanding rigidity and light weight. For these reasons, it is also used in bicycle frames and sailboard masts.

Its excellent tensile strength makes Kevlar®, in combination with polyethylene terephthalate, PET, ideal for making sail fabrics for racing yachts or as puncture-proof protection in all-terrain tyres.

YOUNG PEOPLE

With materials such as acrylonitrile-butadiene-styrene, ABS, and polyamide, PA, sports equipment like skis and skate boards can be given attractive finishes. Kevlar® is also used in high performance sports equipment (see Box 5.5).

In the area of water sports, carbon fibre or glass fibre reinforced epoxy composites are now widely used in equipment used in competitive events as they guarantee rigidity and resistance to fatigue. For yachts, the preferred materials are glass fibre reinforced unsaturated polyesters.

In conclusion, sporting applications certainly put materials to the test, in particular their resistance to significant and repeated constraints. Plastics, which have now become sophisticated and specialised materials, have captured the market. Sport has been one of the driving forces behind the development of plastics, which have had to adapt to increasingly more stringent requirements (see Box 5.6).

Tennis Balls & Squash Balls

The need

All balls used in sports have to retain their elastic and rebound properties, and strength when pounded against a resistant surface – whether it be the foot, racquet or club, the ground in tennis, or even the wall in squash. The secret of their success is rubber.

Squash balls

Squash balls start from an unvulcanised rubber compound, which includes a complex mixture of polymers, fillers, reinforcing materials, processing aids and vulcanising agents. The compound is extruded into plugs: each plug makes half a shell. This is done using compression moulding, with steel moulds and temperatures of 140-160°C. The shells are abraded on the surfaces to be joined and the prepared surfaces coated with adhesive. When the adhesive has dried the two shells are brought together to produce a sphere. The sphere is subjected to a second and final moulding, heating and a vulcanising process that results in a perfect seam. Finally, the balls are abraded over the whole surface to present a clean, matt, uniform surface, before being washed, dried, stamped and packed (see Box 5.7).

The development of the tennis ball

The earliest tennis balls were made from cloth! About half way through the 16th century, this was replaced by a leather-covered ball, stuffed with feathers, dog hair or wool. Between 1860 – 1875 tennis balls were simply rubber spheres, made in the same way as squash balls. But these were prone to slip on the court and be hard to see, so were

Box 5.6 High performance engineering plastics used in sporting equipment

Hytrel® - an engineering plastic from DuPont

Hytrel® thermoplastic polyester elastomer, made by DuPont, is part of a family of engineering thermoplastic elastomers based on copolyester chemistry (crystalline polybutrylene terephthalate, PBT hard segment with an amorphous glycol soft segment). It is used to achieve energy restitution and comfort in the strap and 'Energyzer' (collar + spring) for an in-line skate. This utilises the same concept developed for cross-country skiing – an 'Energyzer' collar that provides energy restitution during flex movements and at the same time keeping the foot in the best position. Hytrel® was chosen for both the strap and collar for its fatigue resistance over a wide temperature range, as well good creep resistance, high elongation and UV resistance.

Quoted from DuPont web site

covered with canvas or flannel. The first covered balls were produced in 1874: they were covered in three pieces, two caps of flannel which fitted onto the balls, and a centre band which overlapped them. As thicker

Box 5.7 Squash balls

Specification for the standard yellow dot squash ball

Diameter	mm	40.0 +/- 0.5
Weight	grams	24.0 +/- 1/0
Stiffness	N/mm @ 23°C	3.2 +/- 0.4
Seam strength	N/mm	6.0 mimimum
Rebound resilience	Sea level:	from 253 cm
	@ 23°C	12% minimum
	@ 45°C	26% - 33%

YOUNG PEOPLE

cloth was used, the overlapped seams became a nuisance, and this led to the two-piece 'figure of eight' covers we see today. The next development came soon after the 1914 – 1918 war, with the introduction of the stitchless ball, with the familiar vulcanised rubber seam we know today. So essentially a modern tennis ball hasn't changed much since the mid eighteen hundreds, it is still constructed in two parts, the rubber sphere core, and the cloth covering.

The materials of modern tennis ball covers

Tennis ball covering is now made by weaving a wool/polyamide, PA, fibre blend weft into a cotton-base warp. The addition of nylon produces a bulky, long-wearing matt of fibres which enhances the life of the balls, allows spin to be imparted at the moment of racquet impact, has an aerodynamic effect during flight, and increases the friction on impact with the court surface. The optimum wool/nylon ratio for maximum wearing life without sacrificing aesthetic qualities is 70/30 with preferred nylon denier in the range of 6 – 12.

Rugby balls

The manufacture of the modern day rugby ball is roughly the same as the manufacture of the leather ball – only the materials have changed.

Gilbert rugby balls are made from a polyester cotton laminate with a synthetic rubber surface for superior grip. They use a tough polyester backing material (to stop the ball stretching), and a secret formula rubber - polymer sheet outer is bonded to the backing material at a high temperature. During this bonding the surface is also cured, which makes the grip permanent. These sheets are then cut out into panels and are stitched inside out, and turned through a gap in the seam approximately 75 mm long. A bladder is then glued to the inside of the ball and finally the last few stitches are made to complete the ball.

Developing a Gilbert rugby ball

The shape of the ball has been developed using solid modelling techniques. This makes it possible to calculate the most effective aerodynamic features. Each design is thoroughly tested in wind tunnels and other purpose-built test rigs. It is then given to world class goal kickers for testing. High speed video is used to see how the ball reacts to the initial conditions of a kick. Gilbert have developed a bladder which helps to keep the trajectory of the ball true in flight.

Gilbert boots

Gilbert also manufacture a wide range of rugby boots. The outsole is made from PEBAX®, a product of Atofina (see Box 5.8).

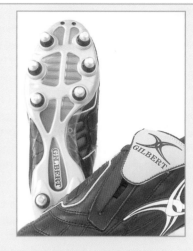

**Box 5.8
PEBAX®**

PEBAX® belongs to the family of engineering plastics known as polyether block amides, PEBA. It is a thermoplastic elastomer, i.e. it recovers its initial shape after deformation. It has all the qualities of the best rubber grades but can also be processed as easily as normal plastics. Their remarkable processing performance makes them an ideal material for components requiring:

- great flexibility (extensive range)

- outstanding impact resistance at low temperatures

- very good dynamic properties due to low hysteresis (alternative flexure)

- very few property variations between -40°C and +80°C

- resistance to most chemical attack.

PEBAX® is widely used in sport where its main applications are:

- soles of football boots and athletic shoes, rugby boots, cycling shoes and long distance ski boots

- heel backs, shoelace eyelets

- vibration-proof components in tennis rackets

- sports goggles

- flippers.

The insole of the Gilbert shoe is polyurethane, PU which maintains stiffness in the midfoot but allows flexion in the toe. The upper is made in one piece from Microfibre (see page 50). This is very light weight, far lighter than leather of equivalent thickness and strength. Further advantages of Microfibre are that it does not retain water, helping it to stay light, and it is stretch resistant, supple and soft to the touch.

The design of crash helmets requires a material which has good thermal insulation and shock absorbing properties. Here the ideal material is expanded poly(phenylethene), PS.

YOUNG PEOPLE

5.5 Young people and health products

Designers of many health products now choose plastics as being the most suitable materials. Blister packs for pills are made from poly(choroethene), PVC, as are bags for liquid drips for hospital use, and blood bags. PVC is chosen for its transparency and barrier effect to gases and flavours in applications where aseptic conditions are extremely stringent.

Medicine or pill bottles need to be unbreakable and have tamper proof safety caps. A typical bottle of pills might have a poly(propene), PP bottle closure, low density poly(ethene), LDPE bottle top liner and high density poly(ethene), HDPE ring seal on a poly(chloroethene), PVC bottle.

The Accuhaler is an example of an innovative health product made possible through plastics (see Box 5.9).

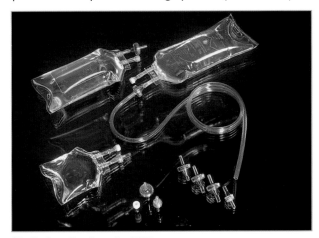

Medical applications for PVC.

Blister packs made from PVC.

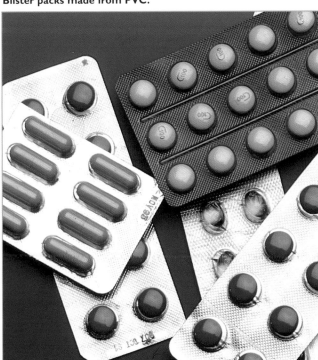

Box 5.9 The Accuhaler

One in three young people will suffer from asthma as they are growing up. The most effective weapon ever developed against asthma has undoubtedly been the inhaler. It has enabled the delivery of asthma treatments where they are most effective, in the respiratory system. But even this crucial innovation is not without its shortcomings. Although the metered dose inhaler is an effective delivery method, if it is not used correctly, little of the dose may be delivered to the patient's lungs. Now thanks to development work carried out by GlaxoSmithKline, one of the world's leading pharmaceutical companies, an inhaler has been created which delivers a measured dose in an easy to use delivery device. The design of the Accuhaler is ground breaking. Its elegant but robust exterior hides a complexity of delicate engineering. This would not have been possible without plastics. The Accuhaler is a Millennium Product, one of the world's most prestigious product design awards.
Source: The Design Council

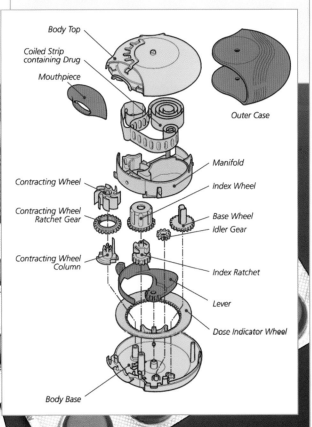

PLASTICS IN THE LIVES OF ADULTS

PLASTICS IN THE LIVES OF ADULTS

Plastics are widely used inside the new Virgin trains

6.1 Transport and Travel

Many adults have to travel in the course of their work. Plastics are equally widely used in buses, trains and planes. In addition, travellers need luggage that is strong enough to survive the automatic sorting machines used in airports.

However, this chapter will focus mainly on the car as in many northern countries, people have come to rely on the car, for getting to work, taking children to school, going out in the evenings and weekends.

As with all technologies, there are positive and negative results. Personal transport is useful. The car protects people from the weather. Many jobs are based on manufacturing and servicing cars, on providing the components for manufacturers, and in processing the plastics and metals from which cars are made. Most cars run on oil based fuels, thus cars contribute to global warming and much energy is used in their production. As more people use cars, the roads get clogged up and new roads have to be built. In the long run it seems that our reliance on cars as we use them today is not sustainable. But in the meantime can a more sustainable car be produced?

The automotive industry is increasingly using plastics instead of metals or glass. This saves energy as cars are lighter thereby using less fuel, and because the environmental impact of processing and transporting plastics is less than it is for metals. The weight issue is crucial: as people demand more features in their cars, there is a tendency for them to become heavier. Plastics hold a key to this problem. Secondly, plastics offer great freedom of design, and allow the integration of different functions within one component – see the box on the car door on page 63. Finally, plastics have a huge advantage over most metals in that they do not corrode. Box 6.1 shows why and where different plastics are used. Box 6.2 shows the proportion of plastics used in cars. Box 6.3 shows the relative use of different plastics.

Design for disassembly

A key feature in car design today is design for disassembly. Current European Union directives demand that any new car is 85% recyclable. Cars have to be designed so that components can be removed easily when they are scrapped, and that as far as possible, components are made from a single material. At present over 14 million cars are scrapped each year in Europe, and 10 million in the US.

Safety

Plastics are used in seat belts and airbags: both are made from polyamide, PA. Bumpers are made from poly(propene), PP and polycarbonate, PC. They are designed to absorb shock and be less dangerous to pedestrians. There are more curved exterior parts. All this is made easier through use of plastics.

Samsonite make their lightweight cases from poly(propene), PP

PLASTICS IN THE LIVES OF ADULTS

Quantities of plastics used in cars

By volume, cars contain more plastics than traditional materials. But by weight they account for less than 10%, due to their lightness. These uses may be explained by the following properties.

Box 6.1 Use of plastics in cars

Applications	Properties sought	Materials used
bumpers, side protection trims	impact resistance, suitability for painting	PP
wheel trims, hub caps	finish, abrasion resistance, rigidity	PA, ABS, polymer alloys, PP
wheel arches	resistance to weather, salt, stones and abrasion	PP, HDPE, recycled PP
spoilers and sills	resistance to weather, salt, stones, abrasion	PVC with plasticisers
roof, tailgate, bonnet, wings, petrol hatch	mouldability, resistance to minor impact, suitability for painting	unsaturated polyesters, polymer alloys
lights, dashboard glazing, reflective number plates	transparency, lightweight, resistance to cleaning products	PMMA
headlamp covers	transparency, lightweight, resistance to temperature, abrasion and stones	PC
side mirror housing	impact resistance, mouldability, resistance to weather and UV radiation	PA
monomaterial dashboard	mouldability, colourability, finish, resistance to scratches and UV radiation	PP
dashboard inserts[A]	mouldability, rigidity	PP, ABS, polymer alloys
interior fittings (doors, seats, armrests, dashboard covering)	surface finish, nice to touch, resistance to scratches, wear and tear, and perspiration	PVC
safety belts	mechanical strength of fibres, resistance to wear and tear	PA
foam for seats, armrests, door panels, steering wheel, dashboard	lightweight, mouldability, comfort	PUR foam
interior finish[B]	mouldability, colourability, surface finish	PP
interior rear mirror housing	mouldability	PA, ABS
petrol tank	impact resistance, mouldability, low permeability to fuels	HDPE
fuel lines	impact resistance, flexibility, low permeability to fuels	PA 11, nylon 11 PA 12, nylon 12
battery housing	inert to chemicals, rigidity, thermal resistance	PP
air vent	mouldability, rigidity	PP
cable and cable sheathing	electrical insulation, impermeability to water, thermal resistance	PVC, cross-linked PE
air filter housing	lightweight, rigidity, thermal resistance	PP
water bottle for windscreen washer	inert to chemicals, mouldability, thermal resistance, impermeabillity	HDPE, PP
headlamp cluster	lightweight, high thermal resistance	unsaturated polyesters
fascia[C]	rigidity, mouldability	PP + fibreglass
vent grill	mouldability, lightweight, rigidity	ABS, PP
small mechanical parts (gear wheels, locks, shock and noise absorbers)	very good mechanical strength, very good resistance to friction, temperature, shock absorbency	PA, PBT, polyaramids, polyacetal, PPS, PEBA

A   Dashboards can be made from either one single material, or from a rigid plastic insert, normally ABS, surrounded by honeycomb PU foam to absorb vibrations, and covered with a PVC coating.
B   Various fittings which furnish the passenger area and cover the metal shell.
C   Unit at the front of the engine which houses various components such as headlamps, radiator, etc.

PLASTICS IN THE LIVES OF ADULTS

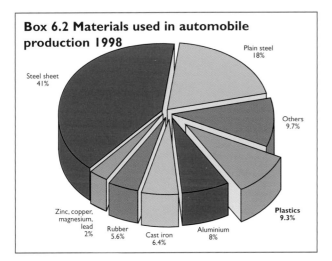

Box 6.2 Materials used in automobile production 1998

- Steel sheet 41%
- Plain steel 18%
- Others 9.7%
- Plastics 9.3%
- Aluminium 8%
- Cast iron 6.4%
- Rubber 5.6%
- Zinc, copper, magnesium, lead 2%

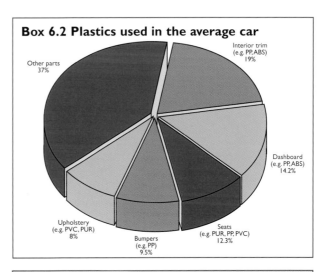

Box 6.2 Plastics used in the average car

- Other parts 37%
- Interior trim (e.g. PP, ABS) 19%
- Dashboard (e.g. PP, ABS) 14.2%
- Seats (e.g. PUR, PP, PVC) 12.3%
- Bumpers (e.g. PP) 9.5%
- Upholstery (e.g. PVC, PUR) 8%

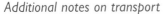

Additional notes on transport

Over the last few years the use of poly(propene), PP, in this sector has developed rapidly because of its outstanding quality:price ratio and its adaptability to specific requirements (see Box 6.4). As a rubber reinforced copolymer, it is suitable for the manufacture of bumpers; as a glass fibre reinforced polymer, its rigidity and thermal resistance are opening up possibilities for under-bonnet applications.

Poly(propene), PP, is now widely used in bumper units, either in the bumper itself, or in some cases also in the crumple zone*. Some wheel trims are also made of PP, although traditionally they are made from polyamides, PA, acrylonitrile-butadiene-styrene, ABS, or a polymer blend. Dashboards in uniform-coloured PP, are also gaining ground. PP can be found in most interior fittings and in composite materials for the bodywork of racing cars. With its good thermal resistance, PP is also finding applications under the bonnet, in the manufacture of expansion chambers, air filters, battery housings, windscreen washer reservoirs, and heating pipes. PP from redundant automotive components is now also being recycled into wheel arches, etc.

* Bumpers are composed of a outer shield and a shock absorbing inner section.

Box 6.4 Poly(propene), PP in cars

Poly(propene), PP, for sheet stamping: the all-round plastic

Embossed plastic is available as semi-finished sheets made up of poly(propene), PP and glass fibre fabric layers. These sheets are thermoformed (heat-stamped). The weight of components made in this way is half the weight of similar components made of steel. Applications include seat housings and seat backs, and complex mechanical components.

The front module of the Volkswagen Golf, which houses 16 different elements including headlamps, the radiator/vent unit, the bonnet locking device, and the air vent grille, is formed out of reinforced poly(propene), PP. Embossed, reinforced thermoplastics are facing competition from long fibre 'granules' of glass fibre reinforced PP, which are processed by injection moulding.

High density poly(ethene), HDPE, has found a key application in car manufacture. It is used increasingly for fuel tanks as a result of the freedom of design it offers due to its ease of moulding. The shape of the tank can be made to suit the configuration of the vehicle, whereas, in the case of metal tanks it was the other way round. Windscreen washer reservoirs and expansion chambers are now also often made from HDPE.

Dashboard made from poly(propene), PP.

Car seats with polyurethane, PU, foam.

PLASTICS IN THE LIVES OF ADULTS

Polyurethane, PU, is an essential material in the modern car: all seat foams are made from it. In terms of weight, PU is the second most widely used plastic in cars after poly(propene), PP.

The three engineering plastics highlighted in Box 6.5 opposite aptly illustrate the progress made possible by employing plastics in the transport sector. The term 'engineering plastics' refers to those which, while costing more than the average plastic, are used for their special properties that so-called commodity plastics do not have.

The sturdiness of engineering plastics makes them ideal materials for use in car components. Polyamides, PA, for example, are most valuable for mechanical parts. They are used for the housing of exterior mirrors and in safety belt fabrics. Volkswagen have started to use these materials to manufacture clutch and accelerator pedals as they help to reduce weight. They are also being used under the bonnet, for example, for the cylinder head covers, air filters and for air intake pipes. Polyamides have now taken the place of both steel and aluminium in these applications.

Mineral glass is being increasingly replaced by polycarbonate, PC, and poly(methyl 2-methyl propenoate), PMMA, which are both less dense than glass, but more easily scratched.

Headlamp 'glass' covers are now often made of polycarbonate, PC, which can withstand temperatures of up to 160°C. As for poly(methyl 2-methyl propenoate), PMMA, this product has a virtual monopoly on applications such as indicator lights and tail-lights. It is also used for top of the range reflective number plates, as well as for dashboard glazing and clear sunroofs.

Glass fibre reinforced polyethylene terephthalate, PET, is suitable for windscreen wiper manufacture. There has also been a rapid growth in the use of quick release

Interior fittings made from poly(choroethene) PVC and poly(propane) PP.

Box 6.5 Engineering plastics in cars

Engineering plastics with an astonishing performance

The polyamides, PA, nylon 11 and nylon 12 are used worldwide for compressed air lines in the braking circuits of heavy goods vehicles. They made their mark in this application thanks to their excellent ability to withstand pressure and their good performance when up against constraints such as cold temperatures, stones, salt, snow, fuel, oil, etc. by far exceeding the performance of steel.

Polyether-block-amide, PEBA, has made very good inroads in the manufacture of small automotive components which have to be rigid whilst being able to recover their initial shape after deformation: aerials, quick release fastenings, etc. Their latest success has been to be chosen for airbag closures; in this application, PEBA combines its attractive appearance with the ability to break on impact, following a specific tear-line, and take into account the airbag's very sudden expansion (20 to 40 milliseconds).

Poly(propene)/polyamide, PP/PA blends are mainly used in under-bonnet applications. They offer clear advantages over polyamides alone in instances where durable dimensional stability is required, as their moisture absorption rate is noticeably lower than for polyamides. An example is in the air conditioning vent.

fastenings made from polybutylene terephthalate, PBT and polyacetal, POM. Top grade engineering plastics, with properties resembling, or even superior to those of metal alloys, have now appeared: polyaramids are, for example, used for door catches. Finally, polyphenylene, sulphide, PPS is used for main water inlet and outlet pipes, as well as water pump turbines.

Composites are making a very modest appearance in this sector: the 4 wheel-drive Golf is fitted with a transmission shaft made of a carbon fibre reinforced unsaturated polyester compound, which is 40% lighter than its steel counterpart. Composites are also used in specialised vehicles, such as racing cars where the light weight of the vehicle is critical.

Transparent and tough polycarbonate, PC and poly(methyl 2-methyl propenoate), PMMA are employed in vehicle lights.

duplicate or decorative image

PLASTICS IN THE LIVES OF ADULTS

Box 6.6 One component instead of 64

Traditional car doors normally house a complex array of parts such as wires for stereo speakers, tracks for the windows, the components of the door locking system. The many intertwining parts make these doors time-consuming and costly to assemble, and susceptible to squeaks, rattles and warranty claims. The plastics company GE Plastics and Delphi Automotive Systems have developed the 'Super Plug™' door module, consolidating 64 parts into one.

It is moulded from Xenoy, an alloy of polybutylene terephthalate, PBT and polycarbonate, PC.

The company states these advantages for the 'Super Plug™':

- 1 kilogram lighter
- less assembly time
- better ergonomics on the assembly line
- easier to service
- 50% fewer warranty claims.

Box 6.7 Rethinking car design - smart™

In April 1994 a group of people set up a company called MCC smart GmbH. That company is now part of DaimlerChrysler, one of the world's largest automotive groups. The people behind the new company were seeking a radical solution to car design. With the contribution of design expertise from Swatch they set about their task. The first step was to question what a car really needs, the effects of cars on local and global environments, and the life of materials from factory, through the car's life, to recycling. The second step was to build a car that's fun to drive, versatile, safe, economical and inexpensive. The result was smart™.

Use of polybutylene terephthalate, PBT and polycarbonate, PC allows for a high surface finish quality. Partly because of its light weight, Smart has good fuel consumption (46 mpg in towns, 66 mpg on the open road). Also CO_2 emissions are very low.

The materials

The basic structure of smart is a steel TRIDION safety shell, to which the body panels are screwed. The interchangeable body panels do not rust, and can be recycled. You can change the colour of your car! More important, body repairs are quick and cheap, as a damaged part can be replaced.

The body panels are made from Xenoy®, a product of GE Plastics. It is impact resistant, and is coloured the whole way through. Thus a slight scratch does not show up: but if there is a serious bang, the panel can be replaced and the broken part recycled. The body panels are injection moulded, which gives better colour matching than painting processes.

PLASTICS IN THE LIVES OF ADULTS

Box 6.8 UK plastic applications

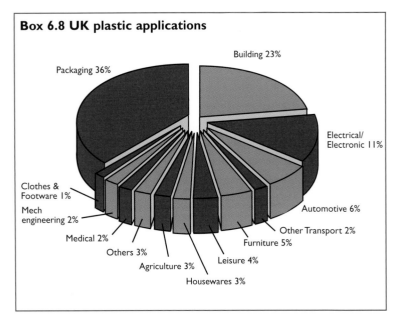

Packaging 36%
Building 23%
Electrical/ Electronic 11%
Automotive 6%
Other Transport 2%
Furniture 5%
Leisure 4%
Housewares 3%
Agriculture 3%
Others 3%
Medical 2%
Mech engineering 2%
Clothes & Footware 1%

6.2 Packaging

Packaging accounts for over a third of plastics used in Britain (see Box 6.8). Why should this be so?

Energy-saving

Plastic packaging saves energy and reduces pollutant emissions both during packaging manufacture and transport as it is lightweight and can be processed at relatively low temperatures. After use, plastic packaging may be reused or its value recovered by material recycling, chemical or feedstock recovery, or incineration with energy recovery (see Chapter 1). Its energy value exceeds that of coal.

Rotproof and virtually unbreakable

Plastics can withstand impact. They cut down the risks of accidents, are safer, and reduce product waste. These properties remain intact during the packaging's entire use as it is not affected by corrosion or adverse weather.

Hygienic, safe and reliable

Plastic packaging protects its contents from external pollution and prevents contamination from microbes.

The increasing use of plastic tamper-proof closures guarantees the contents' quality. Similarly, special caps, which cannot be unscrewed by young children, have been designed for dangerous products.

Transparent

Plastic packaging allows consumers to see the products they are buying and to select them without directly touching them.

Competitive

Plastic packaging is often more competitive in terms of cost to performance ratio. Furthermore, by protecting the contents better and for longer, it cuts down on or may even dispense with the need for preservatives.

Lightweight

Plastic packaging consumes less raw material, and less energy, than any other packaging material. Packs are designed to use less resources. In the average biscuit packet 150 g of food is protected by just 1.5 g of plastics. A supermarket carrier bag weighs less than 0.06% of the weight it can carry. Plastic packaging is easier to handle, and therefore more practical.

Versatile

Rigid or flexible, thick or thin, transparent or opaque, plastic packaging can meet all types of requirements. Shapes can be designed to suit consumers' tastes and expectations.

Criteria determining the choice of plastics

Although the choice of plastic materials for packaging purposes is based on their inherent qualities, other criteria also have to be considered:

- technology (the processing methods suitable for particular plastics, e.g. poly(phenylethene), PS is thermoformed, unlike low density poly(ethene)), LDPE
- handling and storage constraints
- cost
- soild or liquid state, density, pressure
- practicality
- marketing
- shelf-life.

The last fifty years has seen a huge expansion in packaging, which is designed to protect goods from knocks and bangs, from contamination (or from contaminating other things in the home), and from going stale or rotting. One consequence of refrigeration and packaging of food is that less than 2% of food is wasted.

When we go to the supermarket, we find that most products are already packaged. Box 6.9 shows how plastics are used.

PLASTICS IN THE LIVES OF ADULTS

Box 6.9 Use of plastics in packaging

Applications	Properties sought	Materials used
packaging films (e.g. to cover food on trays, such as fresh meat)	some tear resistance, flexibility, transparency	PVC, multilayers (e.g. LDPE/EVA)
motor oil containers	impermeability[A] to water and oily substances, impact resistance	HDPE
bottle tops	rigidity, sealing properties	PP, HDPE
milk bottles	impermeability[A] to water (fresh milk) impermeability to water, flavours and UV (long life)	HDPE HDPE multilayers
bottles for carbonated drinks	impermeability[A] to water, gases and flavours, resistance to chemicals and pressure	PET
bottles for water	impermeability[A] to water, gases and flavours, impact resistance	PET, PVC
delicatessen trays (with or without hinged lid)	transparency, impermeability to gases and oily substances, rigidity	PVC (mainly) PET, PP (to a lesser extent)
films for crisp or confectionery bags	transparent or opaque, impermeability to water, easy to seal	LDPE, PP
ketchup bottles eco-refills toothpaste tubes	thin-walled: resistance to chemicals, impermeability[A] to water, gases, flavours, suitability for printing, sealability	LDPE or PP multilayer PET
boil-in-the-bag/ bags for rice, pasta)	thermal resistance	HDPE
carrier bags from department stores	mechanical strength, flexible film, perforation-proof, visual appeal	LDPE
supermarket carrier bags blister packs (medicines and others)[B]	mechanical strength transparency, impermeability to water, gases and flavours, rigidity	HDPE (high molecular weight) PVC, PET, Vinyl Resin Co-polymers
detergent bottles cleaning product containers	impermeability[A] to water, resistance to chemicals, impact, rigidity	HDPE
yoghurt pots dairy dessert pots	cleavability[C] in multi packs, impermeability to water, transparency	PS PS, PP
cosmetics and healthcare product bottles	matt or shiny finish, smooth finish, resistance to chemicals	HDPE, ABS, PET, blends, PMMA, PA
vending machine cups	rigidity and lightweight, competitive price	PS, PP
bottle crates	impact resistance, ease of injection	HDPE, PP
palletising films	flexibility, shrinkability, perforation-proof	LDPE, LLDPE
lidding films for sliced cooked meats	peelability[D] and weldability	multilayer, nylon, PE
bottles for pure fruit juice	impermeability[A] to fresh juice, impermeability to water, gases, flavours and UVs (long life)	HDPE, multilayer, PP, PET
milk or fruit juice carton lining	impermeable[A] to water, chemical resistance	LDPE
bottles for edible oil	impermeable[A] to water, gases, aromas and oily substances, impact resistance	PVC, PET, HDPE
washing-up liquid bottles	chemical resistance, rigidity, impermeability[A] to water	PET, LDPE, HDPE

A   A 'barrier' property characterises impermeability to a given agent (e.g. oxygen, water, etc.).
B   Blister packs are used to pack batteries, medicines, etc.
C   Cleavability is the ability to break when folded.
D   Peelability is the film's ability to separate without tearing.

PLASTICS IN THE LIVES OF ADULTS

Box 6.10 Multi-layer packaging

Multilayer packaging is increasingly important. By combining the properties of different plastics, it is possible to make a container which is strong and flexible, resistant to oxygen and water, and which keeps the amount of materials to a minimum.

The most sort after quality in food packaging is the barrier property.

Polyolefins (e.g. LDPE, HDPE, LLDPE, PP) are good water barriers but poor O_2 barriers

Polyamides (nylon) are good grease barriers but poor water barriers

EVOH (also known as E/VAL) is a good O_2 barrier but poor water barrier – hence the use of composites.

A toothpaste tube might have five layers:

LDPE	for low cost and flexibility
E/VAC	a tie layer to bond the LDPE and E/VAL together
E/VAL	to create an efficient oxygen barrier
E/VAC	as above
LDPE	as above

A thicker LDPE layer might provide a sufficient oxygen barrier, but it would require more material to produce, transport and dispose of. Multilayer packaging also allows greater use of recycled plastics. Sometimes a product (e.g. a detergent bottle) might be made with three layers of the same plastic (HDPE in this case), with the outer two layers being made from virgin material and the recycled material, which might be of poorer quality and unsuitable colour, in the middle of the 'sandwich'.

Squeezy tomato ketchup bottles are made of 6 layers: one of the inner layers is made from recycled production off-cuts.

Plastics that are most widely used in packaging are poly(ethene), PE, poly(phenylethene), PS, polyethylene PP, terephthalate, PET, acrylonitrile-butadiene-styrene, ABS, poly(chloroethene), PVC, polycarbonate, PC and poly(ethene/ethenyl ethanoate), EVA.

Poly(ethene), PE, is used extensively. It is stable, withstands impact and low temperatures, and is an excellent barrier to water. Low density poly(ethene), LDPE, is mainly used in films and bags (e.g. bags for frozen products) and in multilayer containers either with other plastics or glued onto cardboard. High density poly(ethene), HDPE, which has better rigidity and thermal resistance, is used for hollow containers*.

* Hollow packaging containers are often made by injection blow moulding.

More and more high density poly(ethene), HDPE is being recycled into non-food packaging, such as engine oil containers and detergent bottles.

Poly(chloroethene), PVC, is used to bottle beverages like still or slightly sparkling mineral water and edible oil, as it is impermeable to low pressure gases and flavours, and can withstand oily substances. It is ideal for the manufacture of films, delicatessen trays and display blister packs. It is also used for its transparency and barrier effect to gases and flavours in applications where aseptic conditions are extremely stringent, e.g. in pharmaceutical packaging, in bags for liquid drips for hospital use, and in blood bags. It guarantees full protection of the contents.

The traditional domain poly(phenylethene), PS, has always been for thermoformed packaging - multipack yoghurt pots, and trays, generally for cold storage products. The PS used in trays has to be slightly permeable to water vapour to prevent condensation. It is very rigid, which reduces to an absolute minimum the amounts of material required for processing. A coffee cup made from PS, for example, weighs just 3.5 g.

Poly(propene), PP, is making substantial progress in packaging. It is used for its mechanical strength, rigidity, and resistance to high temperatures, for example, in trays which can be transferred from the freezer straight to the microwave oven, and also as transparent or metal-coated films for the snack food and confectionery market. When used in multilayer structures, PP imparts rigidity.

Polyethylene terephthalate, PET, is extensively used in bottles for carbonated drinks as it acts as a barrier to carbon dioxide and features good resistance to pressure. Its transparency and resistance to high temperatures have opened up new avenues for this material in applications such as trays for microwave ovens.

Acrylonitrile-butadiene-styrene, ABS, is shiny, rigid, suitable for metal-coating and is impact-resistant. The highly transparent poly(methyl 2-methyl propenoate), PMMA, remains confined to use in luxury cosmetics packaging. Polyamides, PA, and poly(propene)/polyamide, PP/PA, or poly(ethene)/polyamide, PE/PA, blends are also used for their chemical resistance. The blends, in particular, are used for their silky smooth finish.

Poly(chloroethene), PVC is less used than it was, mainly as a result from pressure from environmental groups (this is despite the fact that it uses up to 50% less energy than most other plastics to produce.) However, it is still used for bottles for some food products such as dairy products and

PLASTICS IN THE LIVES OF ADULTS

Box 6.11 Advantages of using plastics to package food

APME (the Association of Plastics Manufacturers in Europe) identify eight advantages of using plastics in packaging food.

1. Preventing losses of perishable fruit and keeping it fresh during transport (some expanded poly(phenylethene) EPS containers have a cell-like structure so that each piece of fruit is in its own compartment, which helps to maintain constant temperature and humidity).

2. Lowering food prices by reducing transport costs (a yoghurt container is 1/20th of the weight of a similar glass container).

3. Minimising packaging waste (using plastics for milk bottles has been found to cut down waste).

4. Obtaining more information about the condition of the packaged food – is it safe? (We will see more 'smart' packaging which will change colour if the whole product has been too hot or cold, or if potentially dangerous bacteria are present).

5. Meeting the rapid growth in demand for pre-packed fresh food produce (micro-perforated films are appearing which allow the product to 'breathe': different films can be made according to the storage requirements of the particular product).

6. Increasing the shelf life of packaged food thereby reducing product losses. Modified atmosphere packaging or MAP allows the atmosphere inside the package to suit the specific requirements of the fresh food. Salads benefit from a high oxygen atmosphere. Fresh, red meat also needs oxygen to keep its red bloom, and CO_2 (to inhibit bacterial growth).

7. Reducing the cost of fresh and pre-cooked food (this is becoming increasingly automated: new multilayer films make this possible because of their strength).

8. Increasing shelf life and food safety (made possible by modified atmosphere packaging or MAP to minimise microbial attack by bacteria such as Salmonella or Listeria).

Source: APME web site

edible oils, and in bottles and tubes for non-food products such as toiletries, cosmetics and shampoo. It is also widely used for medical products (see page 55), and in blister packs for medical devices, pharmaceutical products, and hardware.

Solid polycarbonate, PC is used to make re-usable bottles and medical packaging which can be sterilised. PC film is used for pre-baked bread, biscuits, confectionery, meat and processed cheese.

E/VAL (also referred to as ethylene vinyl alcohol, EVOH) is used in multilayer flexible and rigid packaging to provide an oxygen barrier (see Box 6.10).

Box 6.11 summarises current trends and some of the advantages of using plastics for packaging food.

6.3 Plastics at work

The working environment is central to the lives of many adults, for whom the desktop and laptop computers have become essential. Today, most computer users are connected to the Internet. For this we need instant access to servers around the world, to email connections and to other people on the phone. Although much information is conveyed by microwave or radio signals, computer and telephone interconnectivity stills requires a huge infrastructure of cables, which have to be insulated in a material that is durable, flexible and easily coloured so that electricians know which wire is which. Here the main plastics used are poly(ethene/ethenyl ethanoate), EVA, poly(chloroethene), PVC and low density poly(ethene),

LDPE. Fibre optic cables have to be spliced together in enclosures that have high impact performance, dimensional stability and creep resistance, that are resistant to fire and UV and chemicals. These enclosures are made from plastics such as polybutylene terephthalate, PBT, polycarbonate/polybutylene terephthalate, PC/PBT alloy and acrylate-styrene-acrylonitrite, ASA. Telecommunications companies need materials that will be stable under extreme conditions (see Box 6.12).

Laptop computers

Plastics are widely used in laptop computers. The casing is made from acrylonitrile-butadiene-styrene, ABS, or a polycarbonate PC/ABS mixture.

PLASTICS IN THE LIVES OF ADULTS

The screen is made from silicone sandwiched between very thin layers of glass. Printed circuit boards are made from polyester imide, PEI, or polymethyl pentene, PMP. Cables are insulated with poly(ethene), PE, or poly(chloroethene), PVC. Users want their laptops to be as light and robust as possible. The availability of plastics continues to help in this respect.

Office furniture

People need office furniture that is durable and easy to maintain. Many desk tops and work surfaces are made from melamine, which is part of the group of methanal (formaldehyde) polymers.

Melamine resins combine the best properties of phenolic and carbamide resins. They are stable to heat, light and moisture and are colourless. The polymer absorbs colours easily and the powder can be moulded under pressure. Some worktops are made using a cheaper phenolic resin to form the base, which is then coated with a more expensive melamine surface.

Specialist tools

Most professions and trades require specialist tools – many of these are made from plastics.

Designers' drawing equipment is made largely from plastics.

Plastics are replacing wood in many products. These chisel handles, made from poly(propene), PP, can withstand the impact of a hammer blow better than their wooden predecessors.

PLASTICS IN THE LIVES OF ADULTS

Specialist clothing

Some jobs require specialist clothing. Kevlar®, a polyaramid, is used in layers for making bullet-proof vests, flak jackets, anti-knife vests and fragmentation jackets. It is five times stronger than steel, and so is ideal for making police vests and personal armour (see Box 6.13). As people get better at sports, they need more specialist equipment and clothing. This can be in any sport from swimming, motor racing or football (see Box 6.14).

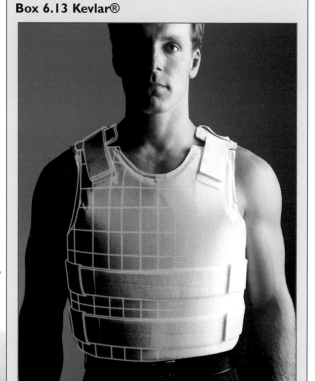

Box 6.13 Kevlar®

Kevlar® body armour

Jim Edwards Jr. of York City Racing Team © *Kelvin Fagan*

Kevlar® gloves

This fire-fighter's suit is made from a fabric containing a polymer very similar to melamine. The fabric is then aluminised and provides protection from flames.

PLASTICS IN THE LIVES OF ADULTS

Box 6.14 Goalkeeper's gloves

Fingersave Es³

The Fingersave goalkeeper's gloves

The need

Goalkeepers in football need a specialist glove, which will:

- keep their hands and fingers warm and supple
- increase performance level, so that the fingers have maximum possible power when saving a hard-kicked ball
- avoid injury if the ball hits the fingers at an angle for which the bones cannot absorb the impact
- look good
- be hard wearing.

The Fingersave solution

adidas, the sports equipment manufacturer, launched their Fingersave goalkeeper's gloves in 1995. The innovation was to integrate spines into the glove: this guarantees flexibility in the forward direction giving greater control, and absorbs impact in the backward direction.

The materials

In each case the palms with spines are made from foamed poly(ethene), PE. The backs of the gloves are made from latex foam with embossed polyurethane, PU. There is an elastic 'bandage' around the wrist made from knitted rubber with polyester to hold the glove firmly in place.

New developments

adidas is currently further developing Fingersave technology, both to simplify the construction and to see if there are possibly better materials for the spines. The Es³ technology currently being developed by adidas in Germany differs from Es² foam in that the colour powder has been removed from the manufacturing process, thereby creating a less dense, more adhesive foam. This enables goalkeepers to enjoy a better feel and grip on the ball. A revised vulcanisation process enhances this. Es³ technology was tested during 2001 by Fabien Barthez, Oliver Kahn and Edwin van der Sar, and introduced into the adidas product range in 2002.

Other developments include adding titanium shards to the foam during the manufacturing process. This leads to 10 – 12% better adhesive properties and makes the foam much more durable. The titanium foam palm is popular with professional goalkeepers, especially those playing or training in dry climates and on hard grounds or artificial turf. A cheaper alternative for increasing durability is embedding carbon fibres into the foam.

The Fingersave Young Pro

Manufacturing processes

The component with the spines on the palms of the gloves is injection moulded. Compression moulding – a combination of heat and pressure – is used to form the latex on the back of the gloves. This is then cut to shape, and layered next to the embossed polyurethane, PU. The different components are joined by a combination of stitching and moulding.

PLASTICS IN THE LIVES OF ADULTS

The wetsuit

Water sport enthusiasts need to be kept warm. In Britain, sea temperatures do not allow surfers to stay in without special protection – the wetsuit. The main material used in wetsuits is 'Neoprene', a synthetic rubber (see Box 6.15). It is a 'closed cell' material which means that it is filled with thousands of tiny gas bubbles, that make the material non-porous and give it its spongy feel and insulating properties. The Neoprene might have a bonded titanium coating to reflect radiated body heat, which reduces energy loss and can increase performance. Sometimes the Neoprene is lined on the inside with nylon fabric, which gives extra strength and makes it easier to get in and out of the wetsuit. It also provides extra warmth. The non-porous Neoprene can also be sandwiched between two layers of nylon. This makes it stronger, but also more prone to wind-chill as the outer nylon can absorb water.

Box 6.15 Neoprene

Neoprene polychloroprene (poly(2-chlorobuta-1,3-diene)) is an extremely versatile synthetic rubber with 70 years of proven performance in a broad industry spectrum. It was originally developed as an oil-resistant substitute for natural rubber. Neoprene is noted for a unique combination of properties, which has led to its use in thousands of applications in diverse environments.

The advantages of Neoprene:

*   resists degradation from sun, ozone and weather
*   performs well in contact with oils and many chemicals
*   remains useful over a wide temperature range
*   displays outstanding physical toughness
*   resists burning inherently better than exclusively hydrocarbon rubbers
*   outstanding resistance to damage caused by flexing and twisting.

The basic chemical composition of Neoprene synthetic rubber is polychloroprene. The polymer structure can be modified by co-polymerizing chloroprene with sulfur and/or 2,3 dichloro-1,3-butadiene to yield a family of materials with a broad range of chemical and physical properties. By proper selection and formulation of these polymers, the compounder can achieve optimum performance for a given end-use.

New developments

Yamamoto, a leading manufacturer of neoprene wetsuits for over 40 years, has improved wetsuit comfort and performance through the addition of precisely controlled amounts of 'Spherical Carbon' and 'FE Polymer'. According to the manufacturer, this disperses force loads of both stretch and compression in a uniform way, and prevents 'self-curing'. The result is three dimensional stress dispersion across the whole of the material, as opposed to the build up of stress at the point of stretch found in regular types of neoprene. The thickness of the material at the point of stretch is also maintained, ensuring maximum thermal protection as well as comfort.

Sources: DuPont, DOW Elastomers and Spartan web sites

PLASTICS IN THE LIVES OF ADULTS

6.4 Plastics in the home

Plastics are widely used in the home. The designers of many modern appliances, such as vacuum cleaners or kettles, have chosen plastics rather than the metals that were common in the past. Plastics have a better strength:weight ratio. They can be formed into a wide variety of shapes. They can be selected for their thermal properties and resistance to abrasion, as well as ability to take colour and other aesthetic properties. The revolutionary design of the Dyson dual-cyclone vacuum-cleaners exploits the properties of different plastics (see below).

The electric kettle

Traditionally kettles were made from metal, usually steel. Russell Hobbs jug kettles are typically made from 10% talc filled poly(propene), PP, with nylon mesh being used for the filter. Polycarbonate, PC, is reasonably priced, can give a good surface finish, and is stable up to temperatures higher than the boiling point of water. It is also kinder to the moulding tools, thereby allowing for very long production runs.

Some kitchen knife handles are made from Delrin®, a DuPont acetal product which bridges the gap between metals and ordinary plastics with a unique combination

Box 6.17 DuPont Crastin® PBT

DuPont Crastin® polybutylene terephthalate, PBT thermoplastic polyester resins are based on polybutylene terephthalate. By making physical and chemical modifications, a very wide range of products is available that are ideally suited to an enormous variety of industrial applications, including electronics, electrical, automotive, mechanical engineering, chemical and apparatus engineering, domestic and medical appliances and sporting goods. In fact, this growing family is currently available in over 30 different grades, approximately half of which are flame retardant.

Among the many features of various Crastin® polybutylene terephthalate, PBT grades are mechanical and physical properties of stiffness and toughness, heat resistance, friction and wear resistance, excellent surface finishes and good colourability. They have excellent electrical insulation characteristics and high arc-resistant grades are available. Processing is simple, with good flow properties leading to short cycle times using standard injection moulding machines. Post-moulding operations such as welding, fastening and gluing are also easy, as are printing, painting, hot stamping and laser marking.

Source: DuPont web site

of strength, stiffness, hardness, dimensional stability, toughness, fatigue resistance, solvent and fuel resistance, abrasion resistance, low wear and low friction. The moulded handle exhibits excellent surface appearance, and is dishwasher safe.

Brauns' iron skirt and connector are made from Crastin® polybutylene terephthalate, PBT (see Box 6.17). This was chosen for its good combination of temperature resistance, flatness, colour stability and low density. The water pump, sprayer parts, push button, cable guide and pivot are made from Delrin®, an acetal resin that is used for its good stiffness and low coefficient of friction. The self-cleaning needle is made from Zytel® HTN, a high performance polyamide, PA that is used for its high heat distortion temperature and easy moulding compared to alternative materials.

**The Dyson
vacuum cleaner**

PLASTICS IN THE LIVES OF ADULTS

6.5 Plastics in buildings and interiors

Plastics are widely used in construction, both of houses and larger buildings (see Boxes 6.18, 6.19).

The building sector is a very large consumer of plastics: with 17% of overall European consumption, it comes second after packaging. Although plastics represent a mere 1% of construction materials in tonnage, they account, in terms of cost, for some 10% of all purchases of construction materials.

Plastics are used in construction in the following areas.

PVC windows: minimum maintenance

PVC has more applications in the building industry than any other plastic. Window frames made from this material, which represented just 5% of all applications 10 years ago, have increased their market share significantly. PVC frames combine the benefits of good thermal insulation and remarkable durability.

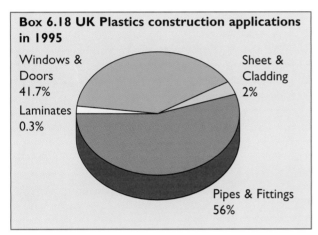

Box 6.18 UK Plastics construction applications in 1995

Windows & Doors 41.7%
Laminates 0.3%
Sheet & Cladding 2%
Pipes & Fittings 56%

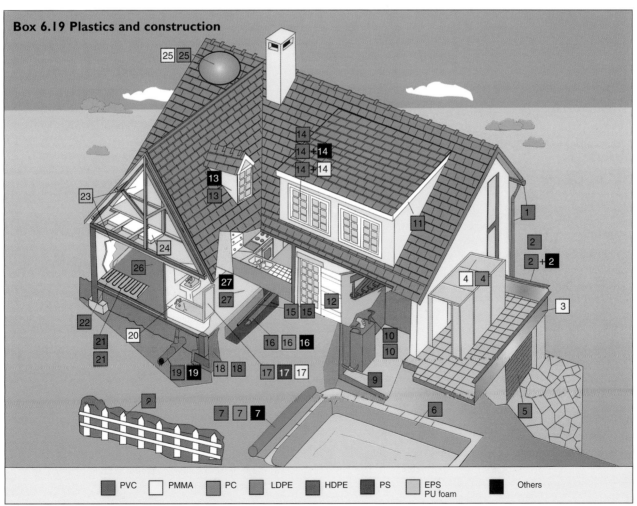

Box 6.19 Plastics and construction

Legend: PVC | PMMA | PC | LDPE | HDPE | PS | EPS PU foam | Others

The numbers on the diagram refer to the numbers in brackets in the table on the following page.

PLASTICS IN THE LIVES OF ADULTS

These uses may be explained by the following properties.

Applications	Properties sought	Materials used
guttering (1)	low noise, stay clean, durability, withstands sunlight	PVC
drainpipes and shoes[A] drain pipe spout (1)	low noise, stay clean, durability, good mechanical properties, rigid, weather resistant	PVC
handrail (2)	decorative, smooth finish	PVC, PVC-PA
balcony wall (3)	attractive, impact resistance	PMMA
conservatory (4)	transparency, impact resistance, no weathering	PMMA, PC
roller shutter (5)	rigidity, smooth finish, low noise	PVC
swimming pool lining (6)	waterproof, durability, decorative	PVC
swimming pool cover (7)	flexibility, rotproof	LDPE, PVC-coated PET, PVC
fences (2)	attractive, impact resistance, durability	PVC
gas pipes (9)	impermeable to gas, durability, impact resistance, waterproof	HDPE
water pipes (10), (15)	resistance to pressure, non toxic, durability, lightweight, no scale deposit	PVC, HDPE (cold water) (15) HDPE, chlorinated PVC (hot water) (10)
soffit boards[B] (11)	good weather ability, rigid, decorative	PVC
shutters (shutters, blinds) (12)	good impact resistance, high mechanical properties, durability	PVC
cladding[C] (13)	waterproof, decorative, durability, easily coloured, thermoformable in situ	PVC, ABS-PVDF
windows (14)	draught and waterproof, thermal insulation, decorative, very good mechanical strength	PVC, PVC-PA, PVC-PMMA
electric cable insulating sheathing (16)	durability, waterproof, flexibility, easily coloured	EVA, PVC, LDPE
shower screen (17)	attractive, rigid, waterproof, impact resistance	PS, PMMA, PC
waterproofing film (floor and under roof) (18)	rotproof, weldability, flexibility, durability	LDPE, PVC
waste pipes (19)	lightweight, easy to install, impact resistance, effluent does not adhere to it	PVC, PP
toilet and bathroom fixtures (20)	comfortable, rigid, low noise, attractive, lightweight	PMMA
under-floor heating pipes (21)	heat resistance, waterproof, easy to install, no scale deposit	HDPE, chlorinated PVC
skirting boards (22)	good impact resistance, electrical insulation	PVC
insulating lining, under-roof panels (23)	high thermal insulation coefficient, lightweight, durability	extruded EPS
case-bays[D] (24)	mouldable, lightweight, rigidity, little compression, insulating	EPS
skylight (25)	transparency, impact resistance	PMMA, PC
floor covering (26)	attractive, withstands wear and tear, easy to clean, bacteria-proof	PVC
bathroom floor tiles (27)	attractive, withstands wear and tear, waterproof, easy to clean, bacteria-proof	PVC, EVA
textile floor covering *	abrasion-proof, range of colours, can be printed, washable	PP, PA

A   shoes connect gutters to waste pipes

B   decorative board edging window or roof

C   decorative protective panels covering another surface

D   fitted in space between girders as under-floor insulation

*   this application is not shown in the diagram

PLASTICS IN THE LIVES OF ADULTS

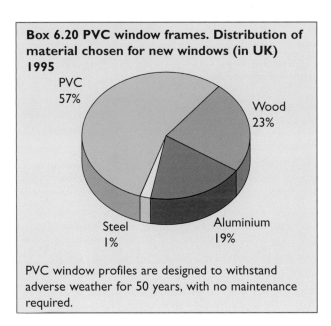

Box 6.20 PVC window frames. Distribution of material chosen for new windows (in UK) 1995

PVC 57%
Wood 23%
Steel 1%
Aluminium 19%

PVC window profiles are designed to withstand adverse weather for 50 years, with no maintenance required.

Today in the UK, 110 000 tonnes per annum of PVC is used in this application (see Box 6.20).

Finally, ease of processing and attractive surface finishes help make poly(chloroethene) PVC highly competitive.

Taming electricity

One area where plastics play a vital role is electric cable insulation. Poly(chloroethene), PVC, low density poly(ethene), LDPE, and poly(ethene/ethenyl ethanoate), EVA, between them share virtually the entire electric cable sheathing and insulation market.

Bacteria-proof pipes

Poly(chloroethene), PVC, and high density poly(ethene), HDPE, are used in 55% of all pipe applications, mainly

for the transportation of clean water and waste water. Chlorinated PVC (extra chlorine atoms are added to the PVC chain by radical reactions) and cross-linked HDPE are used for hot water pipes. These plastics have also opened the way for low temperature under-floor heating.

Home and dry

Low density poly(ethene), LDPE, and poly(chloroethene), PVC, waterproofing films are used in foundations to keep damp at bay, in some cases in conjunction with drainage systems made of rigid PVC pipes.

Insulating foams: comfort and cost savings

Honeycomb polyurethanes, PU, and expanded poly(phenylethene), EPS, are plastic foams which provide remarkable insulation, and represent 50% of the thermal insulation market. Calculations have shown that insulating a house with 50 kg of plastic foam can save 3 700 litres of heating oil over 25 years. Thanks to insulation, overall energy consumption for heating purposes has been halved in the space of 20 years.

Technical and safety glazing

In the area of glazing, poly(methyl 2-methyl propenoate), PMMA, and polycarbonate, PC, are used primarily in conservatories, skylights and balcony parapets. These materials are lighter and can withstand more impact than glass (this is why PC glazing is found in many sports halls). Furthermore they do not burst and shatter, like glass, in the event of fire. Glass, however, is still very much in demand for some vertical panels, which are more susceptible to scratches and abrasion in general.

Versatility in the bathroom

Plastics are now used widely for bathroom fixtures. In particular, poly(methyl 2-methyl propenoate), PMMA,

A vanity basin made from 'acrylic', PMMA.

PLASTICS IN THE LIVES OF ADULTS

commonly known as 'acrylic', is used for baths and shower trays. Without this material, the present freedom of design, colour and comfort, would not be possible.

Poly(chloroethene) PVC floors: guaranteed clean

Plastics may also be found in floor coverings such as PVC, i.e. 'vinyl' floor coverings, and poly(propene), PP or polyamide, PA fibre carpets. PVC floor coverings are easy to keep clean, withstand disinfectants, and can be manufactured in endless designs. They are therefore ideal for hospitals, especially surgical theatres and for kitchens, bathrooms and children's rooms.

Because unity means strength...

Plastics are beginning to make inroads in the areas of interior or exterior wall panelling and for external walls. Polyvinylidene fluoride, i.e. poly(1,1-difluorethene), PDVF, coated acrylonitrile/butadiene/styrene, ABS, panels are already used extensively. The ABS offers impact resistance and PVDF protection against weathering. Research is currently underway to develop compounds which combine virgin raw materials with recycled materials.

6.6 Fabrics in the home

Many fabrics used in homes are plastic based. Many carpets are made from blends using wool and poly(propene), PP or polyamide, PA. Textile designers use polyesters and polyamides in curtains and furniture.

Adding value to traditional materials

Plastics are used not just in visible applications, but also as protection for other materials. This is the case with the metal structures of the Pyramid of the Louvre in Paris which are protected from ultraviolet light and the weather generally by a polyvinylidene fluoride, PDVF layer.

Finally, many thermoplastic and thermosetting polymers are incorporated into waterproofing and protective paints and coatings for the building sector. Such a surface coating gives excellent resistance to weathering, grime and graffiti. They are also added to concrete formulations to improve application; for example, concrete incorporating poly(phenylethene), PS is now available to improve thermal insulation.

The construction sector is the second highest user of plastics after packaging, and their use is growing the whole time. They are versatile, durable and have low maintenance requirements. They can be moulded or extruded into any shape or form. They have an excellent strength to weight ratio. Compared to many traditional building materials, they are economical. Everyone now needs to think about sustainability:

plastics often have less embodied energy (they use less materials and, being light are economical to transport to the site) and are recyclable (see Chapter 1). An overview is given in Box 6.21.

A new art of building

Plastics are clearly used extensively in construction. Several factors have helped increase their use. First of all, construction methods have changed in the last 20 years. Major construction programmes in which mechanisation was in the forefront and only construction costs were taken into account, have made way for projects where maintenance and maintenance costs have also been integrated in the initial building costs. Finding materials which are easy to install and will last with minimum maintenance is therefore the order of the day. Tower blocks are no longer in fashion; rather buildings can feature more variety, in particular with regard to external walls, and have a richer aesthetic appeal as long as planning regulations are adhered to. Increasingly stricter standards and requirements have to be met, for example, in terms of acoustic and thermal comfort as well as protection against intrusion, vandalism and natural disasters.

In short, plastics have a major role to play in the new art of building, by offering:

- multi-functional materials
- airtight and watertight materials for better thermal and acoustic insulation
- rotproof and pollution-proof materials
- vast ranges of shapes and colours
- cheaper on-site installation, thanks to lighter factory-made modules and components.

Used alongside traditional materials, plastics increasingly enhance the scope for design and creativity by successfully combining essential considerations such as visual appeal, functionality and economics.

The Pyramid, Louvre, Paris is protected with PVDF

PLASTICS IN THE LIVES OF ADULTS

Box 6.21 Overview of use of plastic in building

Main uses of plastic in buildings

The main uses are for seals, profiles (windows and doors), pipes, cables, floor coverings, and insulation.

Piping and Conduit

Piping and conduit are the largest users of polymers in construction and consume 35% of production. Poly(chloroethene), PVC and poly(ethene), PE are used for cabling, gutters and fallpipes, and large diameter pipes for sewage, drainage and drinking water.

Cladding and Profiles

Unplasticised poly(chloroethene), uPVC is used for cladding and profiles for windows, doors, coving, and skirting. Phenolic resin is increasingly being used for exterior cladding instead of timber.

Insulation

New building regulations, to which all new buildings have to comply, require a far higher level of thermal insulation than in previous years. Polystyrene rigid foam is incorporated into panels or sandwiched into construction of walls and roofs. It is strong, light and easy to install.

Seals and Gaskets

Seals and gaskets need to be flexible and easy to install. Made from elastomers, they are used for weather strips, aperture seals, gaskets and expansion joints. The polymers used are chloroprene and ethylene-poly(propene)-diene-monomer, EPDM (which have weatherability, resistance to deformation and retain elasticity at low temperatures), and poly(chloroethene), PVC (in windows and doors, and also as a membrane for roofing and linings). 250 000 tonnes of polymers are used each year as a base for adhesive systems and sealants.

Future trends

The future will see the growth of intelligent buildings and methods such as prefabrication which will move work away from construction sites and into factories. New materials and a range of polymeric composites and glass reinforced plastic materials have implications for structures. Manufacturers have a growing commitment to sustainable development: this means a more thorough life-cycle analysis for all products, which includes careful consideration about what will happen to plastics products after they have reached the end of their useful life in a building.

(Source: British Plastics Federation web site)

uPVC shutters

PLASTICS IN THE LIVES OF ADULTS

Almost all modern communications technologies rely on plastics - computers, telephones, cameras, radio, and TV. Our ability to enjoy a film at the cinema is based on plastics - the film that runs through the projector, and screen (see Box 6.22), the seats, carpets and curtains, even the packaging of sweets and popcorn.

Box 6.22 Cinema screens

The need

A cinema screen has to be large, stable in use but flexible for transporting, and completely smooth. Optical properties are crucial: there need to be wide viewing angles, high contrast, bright pictures and good colour temperatures, so that the light from the projector is reflected without distorting the colours.

The screen should be safe in the case of fire. It must not grow mouldy if it is in damp or humid conditions. And it must be perforated to allow a wide range of sound frequencies to pass through it without distortion.

On the other hand, normal cinema screens do not need to be protected from UV light, as they are only used indoors. And since most cinemas are air-conditioned, screens are unlikely to be subjected to wide fluctuations in temperature.

Sometimes images are projected onto screens from behind – such as the backdrop for a theatre set or in an exhibition. Such screens need different optical properties – being more translucent than reflective.

Harkness Hall solutions

Harkness Hall makes a wide variety of equipment for theatres and cinemas, including screens. Some screens – the 'Perlux' range - are coated to increase the gain (the light that is reflected back to the audience). Their 'Matt Plus' screens are non-coated: the reflective properties are built into the plastic from which the screen is made.

A further range is rear projection screens (e.g. the 'Translite' or 'Polacoat' screens) for which a more translucent plastic is needed.

Materials for 'Matt Plus' screens

Their large screens are made from single sheet poly(chloroethene), PVC. Additives used include plasticisers, colours, fire retardants, biocides and fungicides.

Processing methods

The poly(chloroethene), PVC is calendered into a sheet which is approximately 1 400 mm wide and 0.3 mm thick. Strips are joined vertically using a process called tear-seal welding. There are two stages in this – a join is formed using high frequency waves (radio frequency or RF welding). It is then pulled partially apart and secondary welded to give an invisible join when light is projected onto it.

The perforations to allow the sound through are made from 1.2 mm hole approximately 5 mm apart. About 5% of the total screen surface is holes.

The screen is stretched on a single frame: it is fixed to the top rail, pulled slightly to the sides and then stretched by about 5% downwards before being fixed to the bottom rail.

A rigid, acrylic rear-projection screen

The Harkness Hall 'Fresnel Lenticular' Rigid is an efficient high-gain, rear projection surface. It is a rigid one-piece screen made from a cast 'acrylic' poly(methyl 2-methyl propenoate), PMMA material. The rear side bends all the available light into a narrow beam which is concentrated where the viewer can see it. The front side comprises a linear lenticular array which ensures wide distribution of the light. Fresnel Lenticular is extremely suitable for use in normal light conditions. Typically, it has gain of 5 and is five times brighter than conventional rear projection screens.

PLASTICS IN THE LIVES OF ADULTS

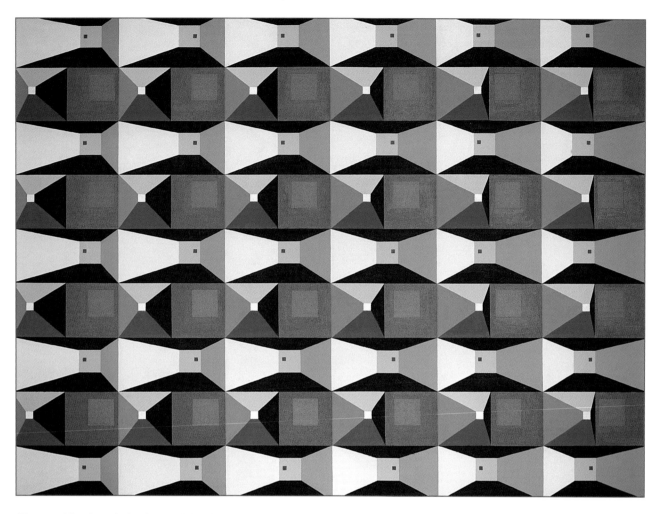

'Transpositions' – painting in acrylic by Roger Ferragallo

The need for self-actualisation

In Maslow's hierarchy of needs, the highest level is the need for 'self-actualisation'. This means doing things that satisfy our need to establish and express our self-identity.

We all express ourselves in different ways. Much painting, poetry, music, dance – indeed all the arts – is the product of people to needing to express themselves, to become who they wish to be.

Acrylic paint is a very versatile medium and can be used in a similar way to either oil or watercolour paints. They came into general use in the 1960's and have remained popular ever since. The paint comprises of water, a pigment and an acrylic binder. As the water evaporates the binder forms a hard clear film. Acrylic paints owe their brillance of colour to this film which reflects light from the pigment when dry.

When used straight from the tube they are very similar to oils, and you can create textured effects. Advantages over oils are that they are quick drying, there is no problem of mixing colours together when you overpaint an area, and the paint stays flexible, allowing paintings to be rolled up; they are also water-resistant. If mixed with water and an acrylic medium to thin down, they can be used like a transparent watercolour. Again overpainting can take place, and as they are water-resistant they do not need a protective layer of glass when framed.

Some traditional instruments, such as the harpsicord, have been redesigned to exploit the properties of engineering plastics. The jacks in this harpsicord are made from Delrin® (see page 72).

PLASTICS IN THE LIVES OF ADULTS

We also express ourselves through the clothes we wear. Many modern fabrics are based on polymeric fibres (see pages 48-51). Some wealthy people acquire status symbols such as boats, which are today made largely from glass reinforced plastics.

LIFE AFTER WORK

LIFE AFTER WORK

As people retire younger and live longer, they continue to use many of the same products as do children and other adults. But with their increased leisure time, retired people have more time for holidays and recreations such as walking, golf and gardening. They will have more time to pursue hobbies such as bird-watching or photography – or simply entertaining friends and spending time with their grand children.

Almost all recreation and leisure activities are enhanced by the use of plastics - from sharing a glass of wine (see Box 7.1), bird watching (see Box 7.2) or other outdoor activities.

A bottle of wine, once opened, needs to be finished before the wine oxidises through contact with air. The wine box is one solution for people who like wine but do not wish to finish the bottle in one evening. As the wine is drawn off, the bag containing the wine collapses and air is prevented from entering through the tap.

Box 7.1 The wine box

The success of the wine box is dependent on the bag inside. The bag is made from layers. The inner or contact layer is linear low density poly(ethene), LLDPE, which keeps the wine in and does not react with it. The outer, barrier layer is a 3-ply laminate of metallised polyester. Its main function is to keep oxygen out.

The outer low density poly(ethene), LDPE is a scuff protection layer, to stop the metallised layer being damaged through contact with the box. The metallised poly(ethene) terephthalate, MetPET layer provides the barrier properties, and the inner poly(ethene/ethenyl ethanoate), EVA is to provide a surface to which the rest of the bag is welded to.

The bag is welded onto the gland, which is made from linear low density poly(ethene), LLDPE.

The tap holder is made from high density poly(ethene), HDPE. Since it is harder than the gland, the push fit is tight. The tap button needs to be elastic, so that it can be pushed to deform many times, and spring back into a position where the spigot is pulled tightly against the tap holder. The tap button is made from polyester-based thermoplastic elastomer. The spigot is made from low density poly(ethene), LDPE. This is softer than the HDPE into which it fits. The handle for the box is also made from LDPE as it is cheap and flexible.

New developments in the wine bag

There is a move in some market areas to replace the outer barrier layer with a 6 micron poly(ethenol), EVOH film, sandwiched between two layers of low density poly(ethene) LLDPE (each 37 microns thick). EVOH provides the oxygen barrier, but is moisture sensitive, hence the linear LLDPE on either side, to provide protection and a surface to weld to. The material is a co-extruded film, using a tie layer to 'glue' the layers together during extrusion. As EVOH does not contain metal, it is recyclable.

Diagram of 3-ply outer film

Material	Thickness
Low density poly(ethene) - LDPE	30 microns
Metallised poly(ethene) terephthalate- MetPET	12 microns
Poly(ethene/ethenyl ethanoate) - EVA (4%)	38 microns

LIFE AFTER WORK

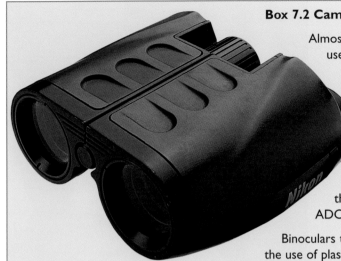

Box 7.2 Cameras and binoculars

Almost all cameras today are made from plastics. They are used in the camera body, lenses (although glass is still widely used) and other components. Indeed, Bakelite, one of the earliest plastics, was used for cameras as far back as the first decade of the 20th century: today polycarbonate, PC is the most widely used polymer for camera bodies. Lenses might be made from PC or poly(methyl 2-methyl propenoate), PMMA acrylic. The liquid crystal display might be manufactured from the thermosetting plastic resin allyl diglycol carbonate, ADC. Photographic film is based on celluloid.

Binoculars too have become lighter and more efficient through the use of plastics in the body – again polycarbonate, PC is the most widely used. Lenses and prisms are mainly made from glass.

7.1 Outdoor activities

Gore-tex

Many high quality outdoor clothes are made from Gore-tex. This is a two or three layer waterproof fabric, which is waterproof, windproof *and* which allows moisture from perspiration to pass through. This prevents the build up of moisture, with its associated clammy feeling. The Gore-tex membrane, is made from expanded polytetrafluoroethylene, ePTFE and an oil-hating polymer (see Box 7.3). ePTFE, is formed into a film containing nine billion pores per square inch. Each pore is 20 000 times smaller than a raindrop, but 700 times larger than a molecule of water. It is completely impervious to rain, snow and sleet and allows perspiration vapour to pass through. The second polymer is an oleophobic (oil-hating) material that allows moisture vapour to pass through, but blocks

contamination from body oils, cosmetics, saltwater and insect repellents that could otherwise affect its waterproof qualities.

Box 7.3 How Gore-tex works

Gore-Tex® Membrane

Outer Fabric

Liner Fabric

Wind

Rain

Body Moisture

Outdoor activities – this woman is protected by a Gore-tex coat

LIFE AFTER WORK

Thermal underwear

The thermal underwear that many skiers wear is made of polypropylene and the fibrefill in winter jackets is poly(methyl 2-methyl propenoate), PMMA, polyester or poly(propene), PP.

Walking boots

There are three main components of a hiking boot: the upper, the midsole, and the outsole. Some boots have an insole as well. The upper is usually made of leather or a combination of fabric (e.g. Cordura) and leather.

The Vibram sole

Thermal underwear helps skiers to keep warm

The midsole gives the boot stability. The midsole offers some of the protection from the foot being bruised by rocks and roots embedded in the trail. This also gives the boot its torsional rigidity. In other words, makes the boot stiff or flimsy. In lightweight boots the midsole is made from poly(ethene/ethenyl ethanoate), EVA, in heavier boots from poly(ethene), PE which is stiffer. The outsole comes in direct contact with the ground. Usually made of rubber, it is identified by the tread, that offers varying degrees of traction. The best-known name for outsoles is Vibram. Gore-tex is also used in walking boots, where again the properties of being waterproof and allowing perspiration out are important.

Good shoes are also essential for climbing

LIFE AFTER WORK

Box 7.4 The Skystreme Location Marker

The need

Whilst climbing in the Alps, Vernon Pascoe was pondering what would happen to him if he was caught in an avalanche. He began to consider some sort of marker – maybe a highly visible balloon that could be inflated quickly. He joined forces with Bernard Hanning, the inventor, to develop a marker which could be used by anyone involved in outdoor pursuits.

Bernie Hanning – inventor of the Skystreme location marker

They developed a design specification. The marker must be small, light and easy to carry, clearly visible, reliable, easy to use and reasonably priced. It must also have a long shelf life, and not rely on external power sources.

Developing the product

To start with, they tried using balloons that could be filled with helium. But this was unsuitable for many reasons. Gas cylinders would be needed. Also helium leaks too easily – the cylinders would need to be replaced too often. Furthermore, wind can blow balloons down as well as up. Bernard, an expert in paragliding, turned this last problem into an opportunity: why not develop a kite that would fly on its own?

The product

The solution was the Skystreme kite. This is an innovative survival aid that comes in a small package about the size of a credit-card. Skystreme is inflated quickly by the mouth and, because of its unique aerofoil design, can float in the air in winds from as little as 4 mph up to hurricane force. Its reflective coating means that it shines when light strikes it and is also detectable by radar. The Skystreme weighs only 43 grams. When inflated it will float in the lightest wind.

The materials

The key to its success is the materials. The body of the kite is made from Mylar, the name of a range of materials manufactured by DuPont. Mylar is normally used for food packaging. In the variant used for Skystreme, there are five layers, yet the total thickness is only 12 microns. It is formed from a biaxially oriented polyester, OPET, film with poly(ethene/ethenyl(ethanoate), EVA, heat seal layer and a polyvinylidene chloride, PVDC, layer on the opposite side of the film from the EVA heat seal layer. In the case of Skystreme, there are two extra layers, aluminium (to make it reflective) and a seal of varnish.

It was only after Hanning 'discovered' Mylar that the Skystreme marker became a real possibility. In addition, it is capable of lifting objects such as light sticks, and the windsock can be used as a thermal vest or inflatable air-splint for emergency situations.

Mylar®

DuPont describe Mylar® as: "The leading polyester film and popular laminating substrate for flexible packaging structures, Mylar® combines easy machinability, strength, high- and low-temperature resistance, crystal clarity, and printability. Plain or metallized, formable, heat-shrinkable and/or coated for barrier, printing or sealing – tough, beautiful Mylar® polyester films offer an outstanding barrier to gas and water vapor, with excellent flex and puncture resistance. The films maintain their strength at both freezer and oven temperatures, for leak-resistant wraps and lidding in a wide range of food and nonfood applications."

Skystreme used a splint

Skystreme used as a thermal vest

LIFE AFTER WORK

7.2 Health

Glasses

Glasses, as their name implies, used to be made from glass. Today many are made from polycarbonate, PC or allyl diglycol carbonate, ADC: the latter has 60% of the prescription lens market. PC is highly transparent, has dimensional stability, is easy to process and has outstanding impact strength.

The artificial hip

Current artificial hip joints are often made of ceramic balls and titanium alloys that rotate in plastic polyamine, PA sockets. Unfortunately, friction between the ball and socket wears out the artificial joints in 10 to 15 years, on average. In a natural hip, fluid surrounds the joint and acts as lubricant. While the same holds true in artificial hips, the fluid does not provide the same level of lubrication. Polymer scientists are currently trying to overcome this problem. They are also investigating the use of fibre additives to diminish the abrasion (see Box 7.5).

Other medical applications

Plastics are widely used in medical applications. They are used in prosthetic devices, shatter-proof glasses and lenses, home testing kits for pregnancy, HIV, cholesterol and blood sugar levels, in digital thermometers, disposable dispensers, inhalers and dosage cups. The contents of any household medicine cupboard are likely to include plastic containers with child-proof or tamper-evident seals, made possible at low cost by the use of plastics.

The main plastics to be found in hospitals are poly(ethene), PE, poly(propene), PP, poly(phenylethene), PS, poly(chloroethene), PVC and polycarbonate, PC.

The properties that make polyethene, PE so useful here are its clarity and ability to remain chemically unreactive. It is used for waterproof sheets, bags, bottles, jars, examination gloves, tubing, caps and enclosures.

Poly(propene), PP is also resistant to chemicals and high heat, and it is light and stiff. This make it suitable for test tubes, bottles, beakers, dishes and jars.

Poly(phenylethene), PS can be found in hospital cafeterias (e.g. trays and plates): it is also used for petri dishes, culture tubes, intravenous butterfly valves, bottles, beakers and filters.

Poly(chloroethene), PVC is widely used in hospitals. It is chosen for its transparency and barrier effect to gases in applications where aseptic conditions are extremely stringent e.g. in pharmaceutical packaging, in bags for liquid drips for hospital use, and in blood bags. It is chemically inert, resistant to water corrosion, and

Box 7.5 The artificial hip

Carbon fibre-reinforced polysulfone, PSU and carbon fibre-reinforced polyetheretherketone, PEEK, are two of several options currently being investigated.
As new fibre reinforced plastics are used for hip devices, the fixation of a plastic hip (stabilising it once implanted to eliminate micromotion of the device and subsequent problems) and the long-term wear will be important to evaluate; improvement in fabrication methods will be a key to success. Fibres may also help to improve knee implants. The knee is a joint that is subjected to high mechanical loads and high frictional forces due to the two articulating, or  rubbing, surfaces. The clinical problem leading to failure is plastic creep and wear. The expected lifetime of a well-designed knee implant is currently about 10-15 years. Once again, a partial solution to these complicated issues may be to produce creep-wear-resistant polymers, potentially in the form of composites.

Source: http://www.ifj.com/issue/August01/38.htm

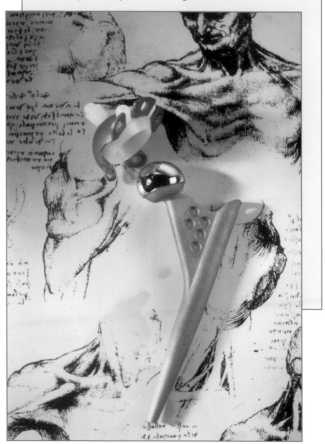

LIFE AFTER WORK

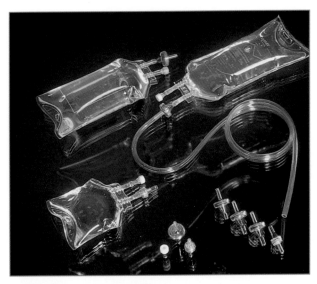

is a tough yet versatile material for processing. It guarantees full protection of the contents.

Polycarbonate, PC is also widely used in medical applications. It possesses a wide range of properties – strength, rigidity and toughness – that help to prevent potentially life-threatening material failures. It can be injection moulded, blow moulded into hollow containers, and extruded into sheet, and thin or thick walled tubing. It is easy to sterilise by ethylene oxide, irradiation or steam autoclaving. PC is used in filter cartridges used in renal dialysis, and for the blood oxygenators, reservoirs and filters commonly used in bypass circuitry during cardiac surgery. It is used also for surgical instruments such as trocars (the long tubes that act as pathways for inserting surgical instruments into the body cavity) and inflators, the syringe-like

instruments used to pressurise flexible catheters during angioplasty procedures. Finally, PC connectors are used for joining flexible poly(chloroethene), PVC components used in intravenous kits, where clarity and toughness are most important.

The technology of sutures has expanded rapidly due to plastics. Suture materials, both natural and synthetic, include cellulose, CE, silk, collagen, polyester, polyamide, PA, polyolefin, polyacrylonitrile, PAN, and carbon. Selected sutures are designed to absorb (to break down in the body) while others are designed to be implanted and later removed; others are designed to be implanted long term. Absorbable sutures are advantageous in many internal applications, where a second surgery for suture removal is not desired.

Trends in health care – an increasing role for plastics

In future there will be important advances in bioengineering, many made possible by plastics. This includes fixation devices for setting bones, where polymers are being developed to replace metal plates and screws which can be too rigid. Knitted artificial fibres are being tested in vascular grafts. Conducting polymers such as polypyrrole are being used in neurosurgery to promote nerve regeneration by allowing a locally applied electrical stimulus. Electrical fields have been found to enhance the regeneration of nerves. This is a blossoming field of textile research interest, since the guidance channel may be a single, continuous hollow tube, or it may be a hollow tube comprised of fibres.

PLASTICS PROCESSING

A designer of plastic produce or a product incorporating plastic components needs to understand both the properties of different polymers, and the main processing technologies. The designer has to work in close collaboration with tool makers and production engineers to ensure that it is possible to manufacture what they have designed. Below we outline some of the most widely used processes:

- extrusion

- injection moulding

- extrusion blow moulding

- injection stretch blow moulding

- thermoforming or sheet moulding

- calendering

- biaxial stretching of film

- blown film extrusion

- rotational moulding

- compession moulding

- glass reinforced plastics, GRP, lay-up and moulding

- structural polyurethane, PV, foam moulding

- rapid prototyping

- spinning synthetic yarns.

PLASTICS PROCESSING

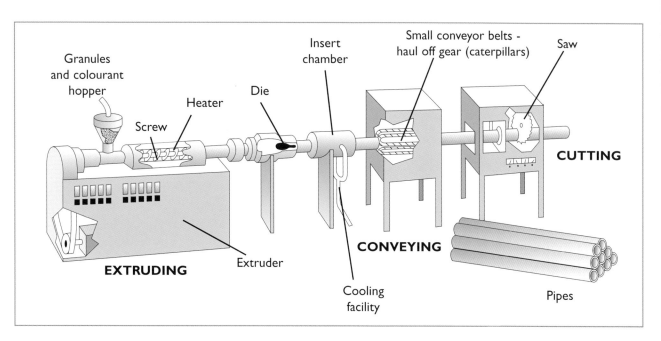

8.1 Extrusion

Continuous extrusion is the process whereby molten plastic is pushed continuously through a shaped hole (profile or die) before being cooled down - typical objects: curtain track, drain pipes, garden hose, guttering, rods, rulers, sheets, tubes and pipes, unplasticised poly(chloro-ethene), uPVC window frames.

The shape of the die determines whether a solid rod, hollow pipe or a plastic sheet will be made.

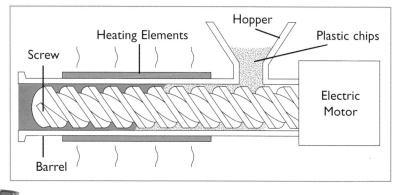

Sheath extrusion is used for making cables. Electric wires are fed through an extrusion line together with the plastic they are going to be coated with - typical objects: electric and optical cables.

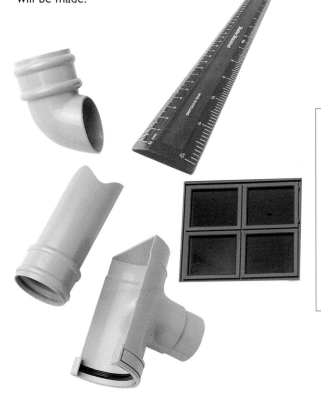

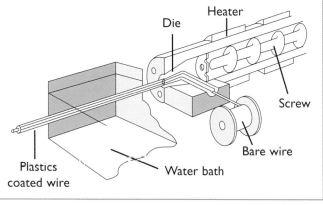

PLASTICS PROCESSING

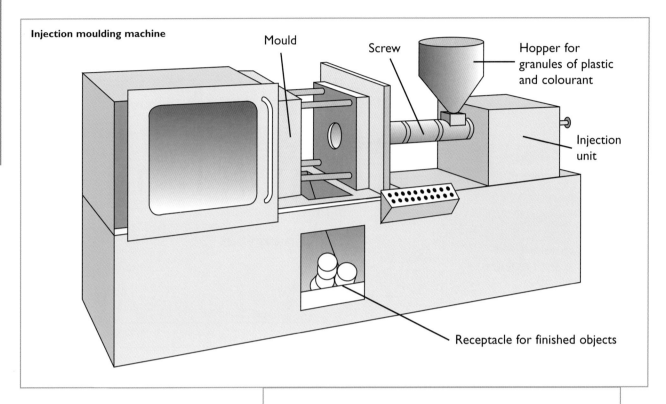

Injection moulding machine

Mould

Screw

Hopper for granules of plastic and colourant

Injection unit

Receptacle for finished objects

8.2 Injection Moulding

Injection moulding is the process whereby the molten plastic is injected into a mould via an injection screw or ram, cooled, and then the object ejected - typical objects: model kits, audio-video cassettes, bottle crates, buckets, car bumpers, dashboards, gear wheels, telephone cases, plastic chairs and washing-up bowls.

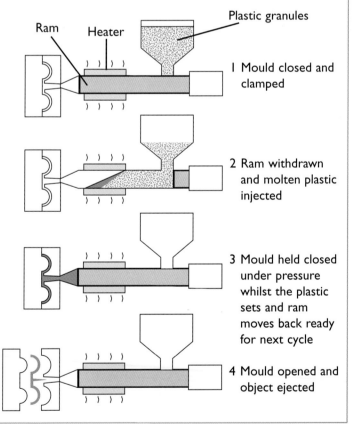

Plastic granules

Ram   Heater

1 Mould closed and clamped

2 Ram withdrawn and molten plastic injected

3 Mould held closed under pressure whilst the plastic sets and ram moves back ready for next cycle

4 Mould opened and object ejected

PLASTICS PROCESSING

Injection moulding machine demonstrated at INTERPLAS 1996. The child's chair is made from poly(propene).
Picture courtesy of Negri Bossi.

PLASTICS PROCESSING

8.3 Extrusion Blow Moulding

Extrusion blow moulding is the process whereby a short tube of melted plastic is extruded and trapped in a mould, then air is blown in so that the plastic takes up the shape of the mould cavity - typical objects: bottles made from poly(chloroethene), PVC, poly(propene), PP or high density poly(ethene), HDPE, petrol tanks, drums.

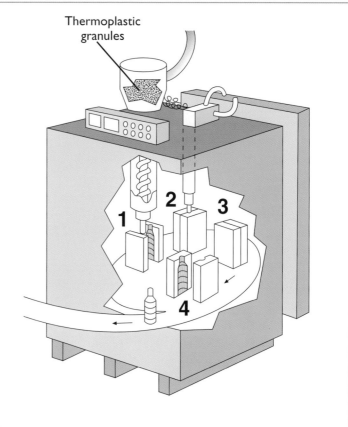

Thermoplastic granules

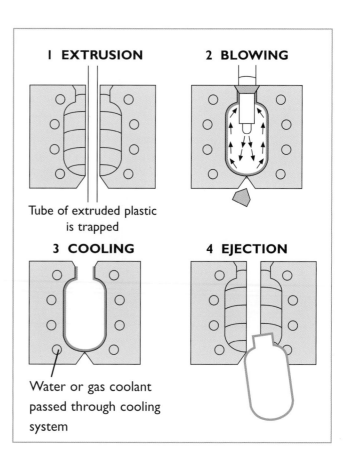

1 EXTRUSION

Tube of extruded plastic is trapped

2 BLOWING

3 COOLING

Water or gas coolant passed through cooling system

4 EJECTION

PLASTICS PROCESSING

8.4 Injection Stretch Blow Moulding

Products

- fizzy drink bottles – carbonated soft drinks

- jars and non carbonated bottles

- toiletries and cosmetics containers

The average fizzy drink bottle contains a liquid pressurised to 14 atmospheres by carbon dioxide. Polyethylene terephthalate, PET, has a sufficiently low permeability to prevent carbon dioxide seeping through it and this makes it a suitable plastics materials for fizzy drink bottles. The strength of PET can be improved by the process of biorientation during production of the container (bottle) in a similar manner to the principle of biaxial stretching of polymer film (see page 98). This produces containers with improved stacking strength and resistance to stress-cracking, which will also withstand the pressure of normal gaseous drinks.

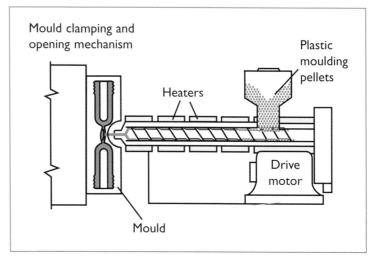

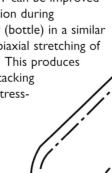

Stage 1

Above:
Injection moulding to produce parisons

Left:
Parison ready for blow moulding

The design of fizzy drink bottles also makes maximum use of designs for pressurized containers in that they are curved on as many areas as possible, including the base. Most bases are now of the *petaloid* design (see diagram below).

Process

The method of blow moulding bottles for gaseous contents is mostly a two part process in order to incorporate the biorientation of the material mentioned above. The first stage is to produce a hollow cylinder, domed at one end, by injection moulding. This shape is known as a 'parison'. The parison is then removed from the injection moulder, re-heated to make sure it is pliable enough and transferred to a bottle mould for the second stage of blow moulding into the final shape. The second stage causes the material to be stretched (oriented) in two directions at right angles to each other (*axial* along the length of the cylinder and *diametrol* across its diameter) thus giving the required strength properties.

Stage 2

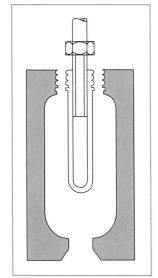

Mould open

With polyethylene teraphthalate, PET parison in position ready for blow moulding into bottle shape.

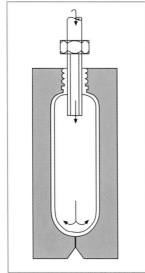

Mould closed

With blown bottle completed ready for removal.

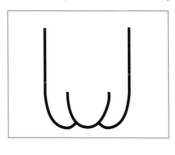

The *petaloid* design of most pop bottle bases

PLASTICS PROCESSING

8.5 Thermoforming or sheet moulding

Thermoforming or sheet moulding is the process whereby an extruded sheet of plastic is heated and then shaped by pressure and/or by vacuum - typical objects: chocolate box trays, refrigerator linings, packaging trays, vending cups, groups of yoghurt pots, baths and acrylic sinks.

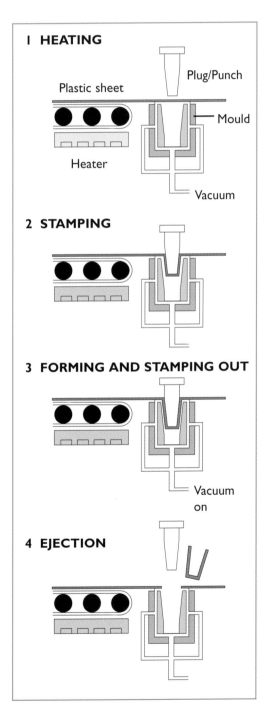

1 HEATING

Plug/Punch
Plastic sheet
Mould
Heater
Vacuum

2 STAMPING

3 FORMING AND STAMPING OUT

Vacuum on

4 EJECTION

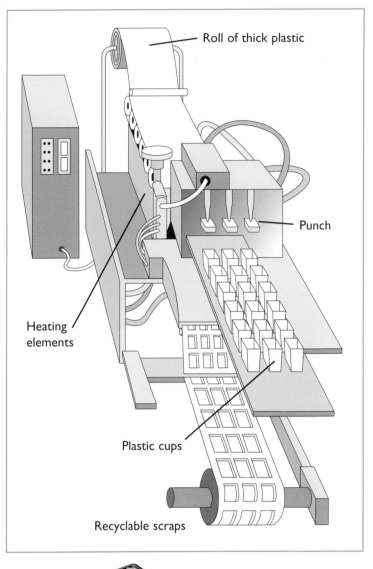

Roll of thick plastic

Punch

Heating elements

Plastic cups

Recyclable scraps

PLASTICS PROCESSING

8.6 Calendering

Products

- protective sheet
- shower curtains
- stretch wrap film
- vinyl flooring
- geomembranes for reservoirs

Process

Suitable thermoplastic compositions are passed through heated metal rollers with progressively smaller gaps to produce continuous film and precision thin sheet. The method is used to produce poly(chloroethene), PVC flexible film in widths of up to 4 metres, and thin PVC and poly(phenylethene), PS rigid foils for use in thermoforming processes or making sheet material. Embossing techniques can also be incorporated into the rolling process.

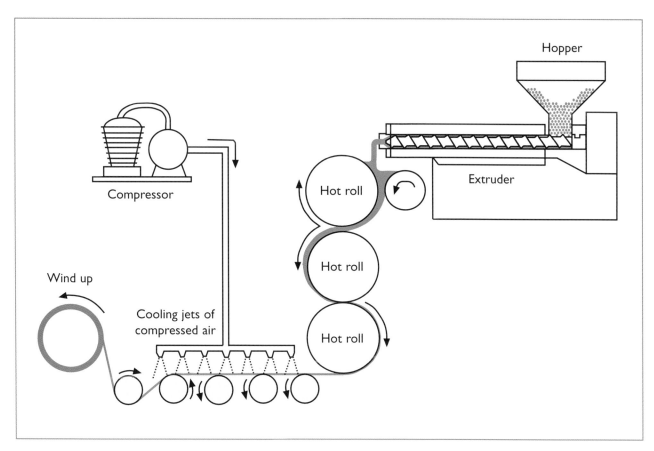

A typical calender system

PLASTICS PROCESSING

8.7 Biaxial Stretching of Film

Product

- poly(propylene), PP and polyester films

Process

Biaxial stretching is the process of stretching semi-molten film in two directions (normally on two axes at 90° to each other) as it leaves the heated die of an extruder.

In the case of poly(propylene), PP and polyester films, crystallisation occurs on stretching, increasing the mechanical strength of the materials and decreasing the water vapour permeability. One production method for biaxially stretched polyester film is illustrated below.

The molten plastic is extruded through the slit of a metal die, producing a hot molten ribbon of film. The hot ribbon then drops on to a chilled metal roller to solidify it and pull it away from the die. The cooled

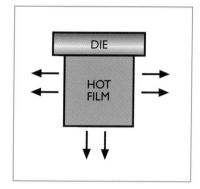

Biaxially stretching polymer film

ribbon of film then passes through an oven where it is reheated and stretched first along its length and then across its width (biaxial stretching). The film is then held in the stretched condition and allowed to cool (set) before being wound into large rolls for despatch to the customer.

A typical production system for biaxially stretched film

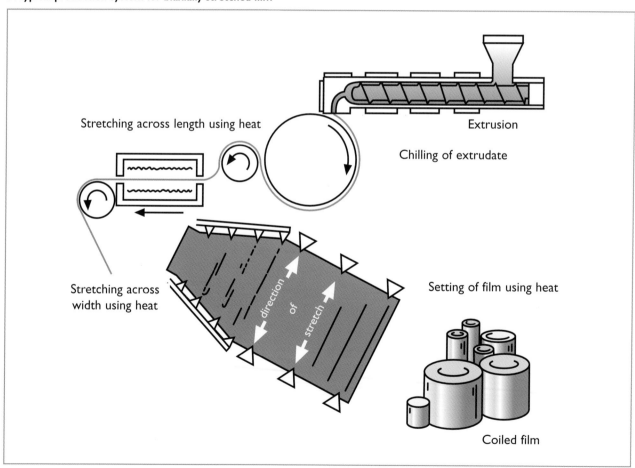

PLASTICS PROCESSING

8.8 Blown Film Extrusion

Tubular sheet or sheath extrusion is the process whereby extruded plastic is expanded into a sheath and then wound onto reels - typical objects: packaging films, 'plastic' bags, greenhouse covers.

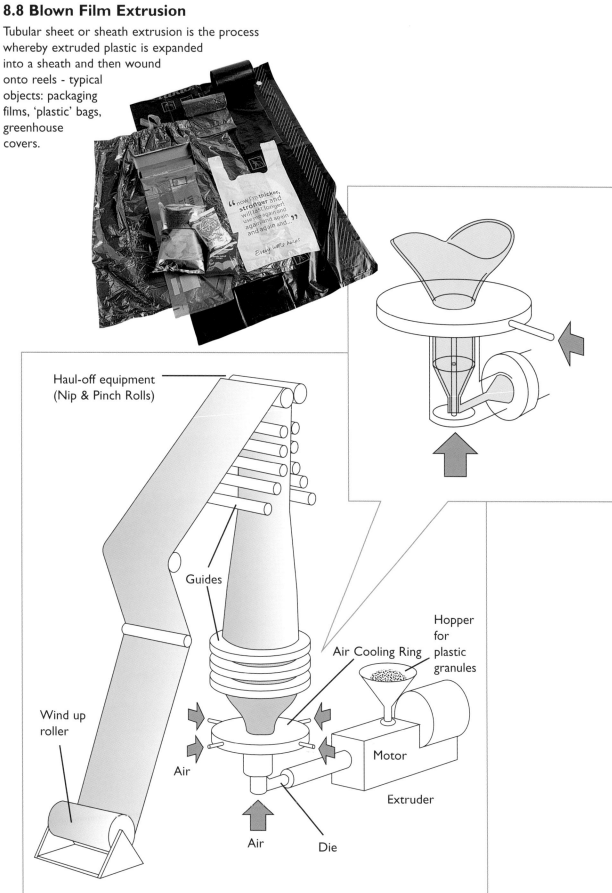

Haul-off equipment (Nip & Pinch Rolls)

Guides

Wind up roller

Air

Air

Die

Air Cooling Ring

Hopper for plastic granules

Motor

Extruder

PLASTICS PROCESSING

Blown film extrusion of poly(ethene), in action at INTERPLAS 1996 *Picture courtesy of Tripleplas*

PLASTICS PROCESSING

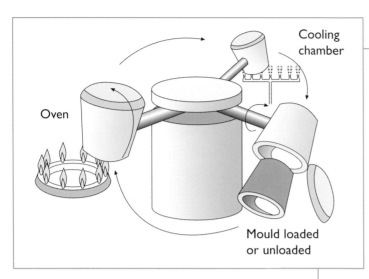

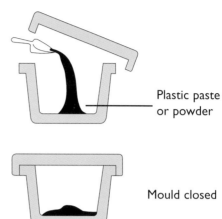

Oven

Cooling chamber

Mould loaded or unloaded

Plastic paste or powder

Mould closed

8.9 Rotational Moulding

The rotational moulding process consists of rotating a heated mould containing plastic paste or powder. As the plastic melts and the mould rotates, the plastic coats the surface of the mould cavity with an even layer of plastic. The mould is then cooled before opening - typical objects: farm tanks, barrels, septic tanks and large hollow toys.

1700 - 270ºC

Heated and rotated

OVEN

Air Water — Air Water

Cooled

COOLER

Object removed

Erica Mitchell, Womans World Freestyle Kayaking Champion
Picture by Dan Gavere

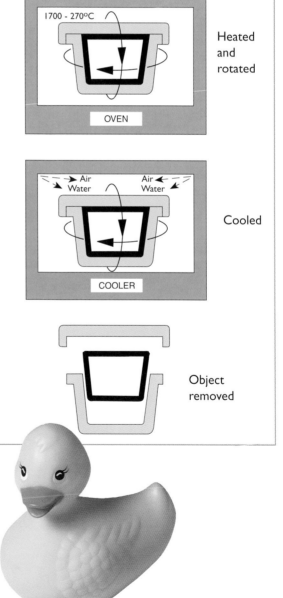

PLASTICS PROCESSING

8.10 Compression Moulding

Compression moulding is the process most often used for shaping thermosetting plastics. The plastic 'moulding powder' is heated and compressed into shape - typical objects: children's tableware, electric plugs, sockets and light switches.

Other processes

Calendering is the process whereby extruded plastic is squeezed through rotating rollers to produce sheets or films. It can then be combined with other materials (cardboard, fabrics, etc.) to coat them - typical objects: plastic floor coverings, protective sheeting, sheets for thermoforming applications.

The cast sheet process, used for example to manufacture poly(methyl 2-methyl propenoate), PMMA, sheets. In situ foam dispensing, for example for filling cavities (e.g. polyurethene, PU, car seat pads, cavity wall insulation).

It is easy to see that the variety of monomers, polymers, additives and processing methods, yields plastic materials which can offer virtually unlimited tailor-made solutions to all our everyday needs.

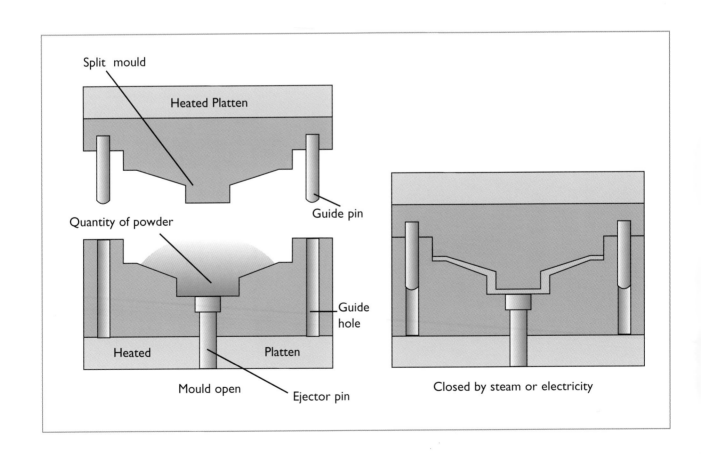

Split mould

Heated Platten

Guide pin

Quantity of powder

Guide hole

Heated   Platten

Mould open   Ejector pin

Closed by steam or electricity

PLASTICS PROCESSING

8.11 Glass Reinforced Plastics (GRP) Lay-up and Moulding

Products

- canoes
- boat and car bodies
- chemical plant
- architectural claddings

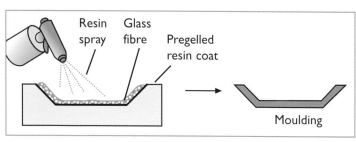

Lay-up technique for GRP

Process (GRP lay-up)

The lay-up technique for Glass Reinforced Plastics (GRP) involves a comparatively simple profile mould of metal, wood or plaster and the following processes:

1. Liquid polyester resin, mixed with a catalyst (or hardener), is applied to the mould to form a pre-gelled coat.

2. Glass fibre in mat or woven fabric form is laid on the first gelcoat and liquid polyester resin/catalyst mix is sprayed on until the fibre layer is saturated.

3. When the resin mix has hardened, the moulding is removed from the mould. Curing (setting) can take place in the cold or can be speeded up by heating.

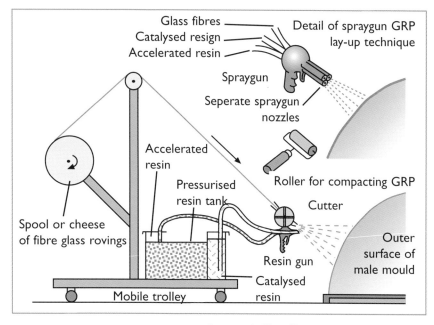

Automatic fibre dispenser and resin spraygun

Process (GRP moulding)

Two other techniques used with Glass Reinforced Plastics (GRP) are the rubber-bag and matched-die moulding methods in which pressure is applied to the top surface of the moulding during processing. Various compositions of polyester resin/catalyst/ glass fibre are used to produce mouldings in both these pressurised processes. By heating, comparatively fast hardening of the resin is possible. The two methods are illustrated right.

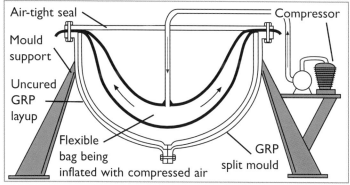

Pressure bag method of moulding GRP

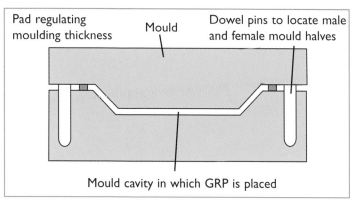

Matched mould method for GRP

PLASTICS PROCESSING

8.12 Structural polyurethane (PU) Foam Moulding

Products

- computer housings

- tool handles

- casings/cabinets

- furniture shells

- decorative simulated wood effects for wall panelling

Process

A two part pre-mix of polyurethane, PU, foam is poured rapidly into a split cavity mould. The chemical reaction of the mix causes the foam to expand rapidly and take on the cavity form of the mould. The foam sets within a few minutes to produce strong, lightweight mouldings. A development of this process is used to make integrally skinned PU foams; a combination of a foam interior with a hard solid skin or surface which can be finished with lacquers.

Compression moulding process

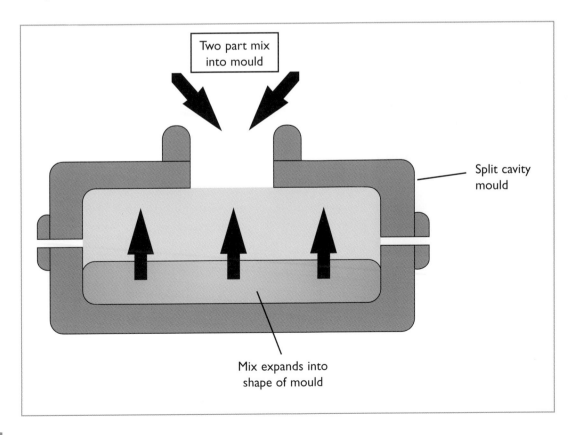

Two part mix into mould

Split cavity mould

Mix expands into shape of mould

PLASTICS PROCESSING

8.13 Rapid prototyping

We include this because of four trends in requirements for the manufacturing industry. Over the last three decades

- the number of variants of a product has gone UP

- product lifetime has gone DOWN

- product complexity has gone UP

- required delivery time has gone DOWN

Thus there is a need for new manufacturing technologies for quick production of short runs, where the cost and time spent in tool making is uneconomic.

Rapid prototyping technologies offer a solution. In essence, rapid prototyping is a CAD/CAM process whereby a product or component is designed using 3D CAD software, from which a prototype can be made using a computer-controlled process. Its main use is in developing parts for testing. But when a short production run is needed, it can be more economical to produce the components using rapid prototyping technology, than to make a mould for injection moulding, or using conventional methods such as NC (numerically controlled) milling or hand carving.

There are currently six main types of rapid protoyping.

1. Stereolithography

The component is built up in layers on the platform. The liquid is a photopolymer. When it is exposed to ultra-violet light from the laser beam, it solidifies or is cured. The platform moves downwards, the sweeper passes over the newly formed layer, breaking the surface tension and ensuring that a flat surface is produced for the next layer. Subsequent layers are laid down, and bind together. The part is then removed from the vat.

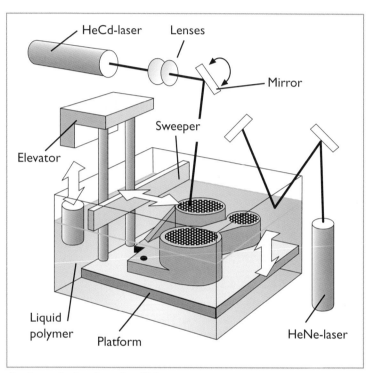

A schematic drawing of an SLA

2. Solid ground curing

This also uses a liquid photopolymer sensitive to ultra-violet light. But here the vat moves horizontally as well as vertically. An ultra-violet lamp is used to 'flood' the chamber and expose an entire layer at once, rather than scanning it. Also wax is used to provide a support structure for the component as it builds up. Each layer is milled to the correct height before the next layer is laid down.

A schematic drawing of a SOLIDER process

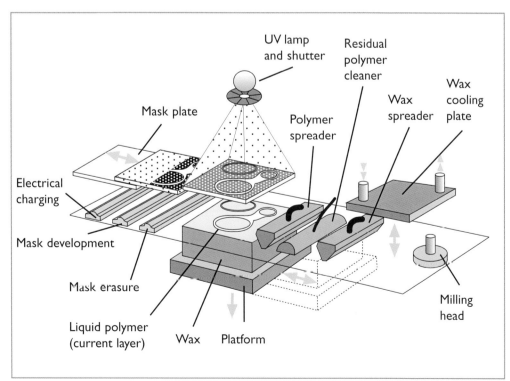

PLASTICS PROCESSING

Rapid prototyping continued

3. Selective laser sintering

This is a totally different process in which powder is spread over a platform by a roller. The laser then sinters selected areas, which makes the powdered polymer melt and then harden.

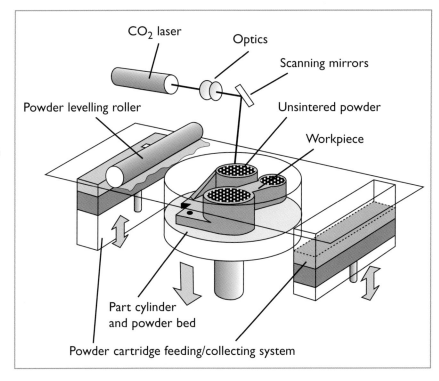

CO₂ laser

Optics

Scanning mirrors

Powder levelling roller

Unsintered powder

Workpiece

Part cylinder and powder bed

Powder cartridge feeding/collecting system

4. Laminated object manufacturing

This method builds up layers from foil. There is a layer of binder under the foil. So when each layer is pressed by the heated roller, it glues to the layer beneath. The foil is cut to shape by the laser.

Laser

Mirror

Heated roller

Optic head

Platform

Feeder

Collector

A schematic drawing of a LOM process

PLASTICS PROCESSING

Rapid prototyping continued

5. Fused Depostion Modelling

The FDM build material is a polymer filament which is passed through a heating element, melted and extruded. Each slice of the model is drawn from a continuous length of the molten filament. Typical build materials are acrylonitrile-butadiene-styrene, ABS, polyphenylene sulphide, PPS and polycarbonate, PC.

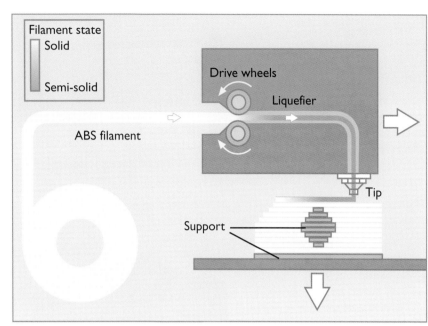

Fused Deposition Modelling

6. 3D Printing processes

Desktop or 3D Printers use ink jet technology to either print binder onto a substrate or directly print models. These processes are typically used for visualisation or concept modelling, rather than production. Sometimes they are used for investment casting: by translating CAD designs into solid 3D models so accurate it is possible to go beyond concept modelling to produce tooling grade patterns ready for casting or mold-making. The main print based processes are:

Solidscape MMII – this builds model in 2D slices, which are printed in a low melt polymer and supported with a soluble wax. After each layer is printed a milling head machines the layer to a precise thickness (normally between 0.013 – 0.076 mm).

Z-Corp – the Z-Corp process is very similar to the laser sinter process, except that the sintering laser is replaced with a print head and plotter carriage. The build materials are typically plasters or starch, rather than synthetic polymers, although the outer surfaces are sometimes strengthened with super glue or resin.

Thermojet – the Thermojet build process comprises of a print head that prints 2D slices of the protoype model using a wax material. Undercuts are supported with thin columns of wax.

PLASTICS PROCESSING

8.14 Synthetic Yarns

Man-made fibres are *either* regenerated fibres, made from natural polymers such as cellulose, *or* synthetic fibres, made from manufactured polymers such as polyamides, PA, or polyester.

A spinneret is used to make synthetic yarns: essentially this is an extrusion die with either very small holes or slits. The shape and size of the hole or slit determine the cross section of the fibre, which affects its properties such as hand or drape. The polymer is heated to melting point, or dissolved in a solution, and forced through the spinneret in filaments. These are cooled to form a solid filament.

There are three commonly used processes – wet spinning, dry spinning and melt spinning (see diagrams).

The filament is then treated. It can be stretched (drawn) and lubricated to give a continuous yarn. It can be partially stretched and lubricated, and then texturised. Or it can be chopped into short lengths and lubricated to give a staple fibre, which is then spun into yarn.

The yarn can then be woven or knitted to produce a fabric.

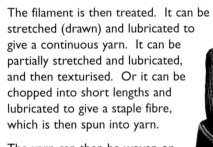

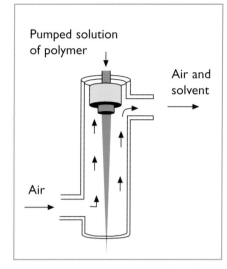

Melt spinning

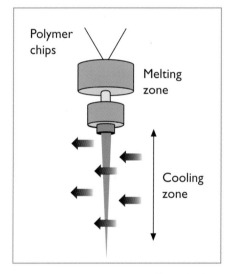

Dry spinning

Spinnerets

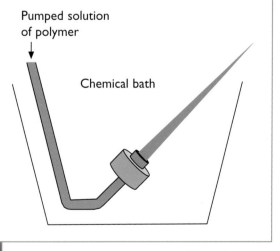

Wet spinning

CHEMISTRY OF POLYMERS

CHEMISTRY OF POLYMERS

There are 4 stages in making a plastic (see Box 9.1):

Box 9.1

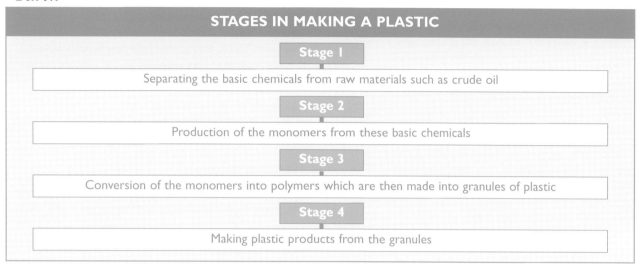

STAGES IN MAKING A PLASTIC
Stage 1
Separating the basic chemicals from raw materials such as crude oil
Stage 2
Production of the monomers from these basic chemicals
Stage 3
Conversion of the monomers into polymers which are then made into granules of plastic
Stage 4
Making plastic products from the granules

9.1 Separating the basic chemicals from the raw materials

As described in Chapter 2, synthetic polymers are made from monomers. These compounds do not occur naturally. They are made from hydrocarbons which contain single carbon-carbon bonds. These are called saturated hydrocarbons. The alkanes, e.g. ethane, propane and butane, are examples of saturated hydrocarbons. Crude oil is the major source of these and other hydrocarbons such as natural gas and coal are also used to a certain extent.

Crude oil is a liquid, which is a mixture of literally thousands of different chemicals. A mixture of liquids with different boiling points can be separated by distillation.

In the simplest case the mixture is heated and the component with the lowest boiling point evaporates first. The vapour can be condensed thus separating this component from the original mixture.

Crude oil is such a complex mixture it cannot be separated by simple distillation into the separate hydrocarbons. In the industrial process, crude oil is fractionally distilled. This is shown in the diagram below (see Box 9.2).

The crude oil is first heated and vaporised. The vapours are then allowed to rise up a tower called a fractionating column which contains a series of trays at different heights. As the vapours rise up the tower fractions, each with different ranges of boiling points, condense at different heights within the column. A fraction is a group of hydrocarbons that boil within a specified range. High boiling point fractions condense in the lower part of the tower where it is hotter. Lower boiling point fractions condense higher up the tower where it is cooler. In general, the higher the boiling point of a fraction then the longer the carbon chain in its molecules.

Box 9.2 Fractional distillation

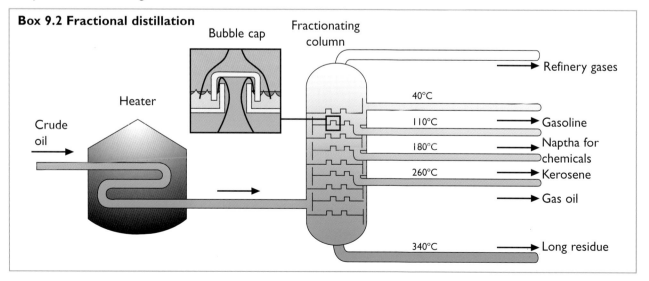

CHEMISTRY OF POLYMERS

9.2 Making the monomers

The chemicals separated from crude oil are mixtures of saturated hydrocarbons together with some more complicated compounds which contain rings of carbon atoms e.g. benzene. So how are unsaturated monomers with short carbon chains made from these?

The greatest demand is for the crude oil fractions containing short molecules. In order to meet this demand long chain hydrocarbons are broken down into smaller molecules, a process known as cracking.

Traditionally the process involved heating a long chain fraction, such as naphtha, to a high temperature. The thermal energy supplied resulted in bonds being broken and smaller molecules were produced. This was called thermal cracking (see Box 9.3).

In more recent times, it has been found that certain catalysts will bring about cracking at lower temperatures. This is called catalytic cracking. When naphtha is cracked a mixture of molecules is produced (see Box 9.4). This includes shorter chain alkanes and also short chain unsaturated hydrocarbons (alkenes). It is these alkenes that are used as the monomers to produce addition compounds (see section 9.3.1).

Simple unsaturated monomers such as ethene and propene are obtained by cracking as described above. More complex monomers such as chloroethene and tetrafluoroethene are made from alkenes by carrying out further reactions.

The monomers for making condensation polymers are also made from compounds obtained from crude oil.

Box 9.3 Flow scheme of the cracking of naphtha to produce alkenes

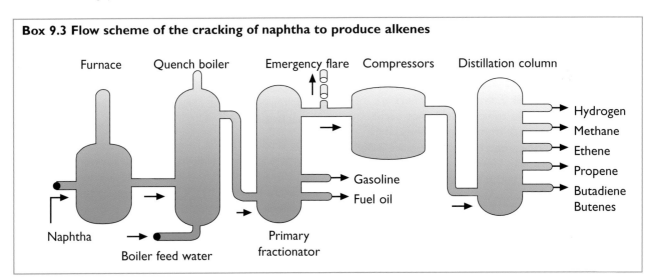

Box 9.4 An example of cracking

One alkane in the naphtha fraction is octane. This can be cracked to give the products shown.

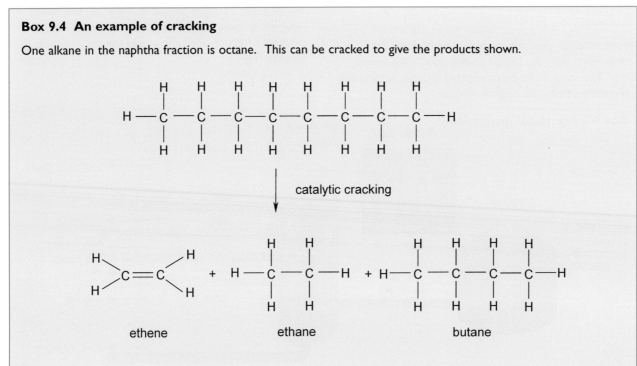

CHEMISTRY OF POLYMERS

9.3 Polymerisation

The monomers can be combined in two ways: addition and condensation polymerisation.

9.3.1 Addition polymerisation

Many monomers are unsaturated carbon compounds. This means their molecules contain a double bond between two carbon atoms (some monomers contain a carbon-carbon triple bond). Under certain conditions the double, or triple, bond breaks open enabling the monomer molecule to link to other monomer molecules to form the polymer. This type of polymerisation is called addition polymerisation. If the monomer is represented by A then addition polymerisation can be represented as follows:

A+A+A+A+A+A+A+A $\longrightarrow$ A-A-A-A-A-A-A-A

Or, more generally

nA $\longrightarrow$ (A)n where n is a large number

The simplest example of this is the polymerisation of ethene. Each ethene molecule contains a carbon-carbon double bond. Under appropriate conditions one of the bonds in the double bond breaks. This still leaves a single bond between the two carbon atoms. The 'spare' electrons from the carbon atoms are used to form a bond to other ethene molecules. As many as 14 000 ethene units may link together to form a giant molecule of poly(ethene), PE.

$$n(CH_2 = CH_2) \longrightarrow (-CH_2-CH_2-)_n$$

The discovery of poly(ethene) is described in Box 9.5.

Other unsaturated monomers react similarly (see Box 9.6, page 114). They can usually be regarded as derivatives of ethene in which one or more of the hydrogen atoms are replaced by other atoms or groups of atoms. The 'backbone' of the polymer is thus the same but different groups project at the sides of the chain. Thus propene, for example, reacts to form poly(propene) as follows:

$$nCH_3 - CH = CH_2 \longrightarrow \left(CH - CH_2 \right)_n \quad \overset{CH_3}{\underset{|}{}}$$

If a mixture of monomers is used in place of a single monomer then the polymer obtained is called a co-polymer. An example is the co-polymer obtained when ethene is reacted with propene. A section of the co-polymer chain may be represented as:

$$- CH_2 - \underset{\underset{CH_3}{|}}{CH} - CH_2 - \underset{\underset{CH_3}{|}}{CH} - CH_2 - CH_2 - CH_2 - CH_2 - \underset{\underset{CH_3}{|}}{CH} - CH_2 - \underset{\underset{CH_3}{|}}{CH} -$$

Box 9.5 The discovery of Poly(ethene)

Poly(ethene), PE was discovered by accident in 1933. A team of researchers at ICI were trying to make benzaldehyde react with ethene. They used high pressures of about 2000 atmospheres. They left the mixture over the weekend to react. Their apparatus had a slight leak and they added some extra ethene. When they opened the vessel they found they had produced a white waxy solid with the empirical formula CH_2. This was poly(ethene). The early work on this process was dangerous as it sometimes resulted in an explosion. In 1935 a way was found of controlling the reaction. It was also found that the presence of benzaldehyde was unnecessary but that the presence of a small amount of oxygen was essential. The leak in the research team's original apparatus had let in some oxygen. If it were not for this the discovery of poly(ethene) might not have been made.

CHEMISTRY OF POLYMERS

Box 9.6 Some common addition polymers and their monomers

Traditional names are given in italics

Name of monomer	Structure of monomer	Name of polymer	Structure of repeat unit of polymer
ethene *ethylene*	$H_2C=CH_2$	poly(ethene) *polyethylene*	$-[CH_2-CH_2]-$
propene *propylene*	$H_2C=CH-CH_3$	poly(propene) *polypropylene*	$-[CH_2-CH(CH_3)]-$
chloroethene *vinyl chloride*	$H_2C=CH-Cl$	poly(chloroethene) *poly (vinyl chloride)*	$-[CH_2-CHCl]-$
phenylethene *styrene*	$H_2C=CH-C_6H_5$	phenylethene *polystyrene*	$-[CH_2-CH(C_6H_5)]-$
tetrafluoroethene *tetrafluoroethylene*	$F_2C=CF_2$	poly(tetrafluoroethene) *polytetrafluoroethylene*	$-[CF_2-CF_2]-$
propenonitrile *acrylonitrile*	$H_2C=CH-CN$	poly(propenonitrile) *polyacrylonitrile*	$-[CH_2-CH(CN)]-$
methyl 2-methylpropenoate *methyl methacrylate*	$H_2C=C(CH_3)-COOCH_3$	poly(methyl 2-methylpropenoate) *poly (methyl methacrylate)*	$-[CH_2-C(CH_3)(COOCH_3)]-$

CHEMISTRY OF POLYMERS

**Use of ABS, a co-polymer of propenonitrile-buta-1,
3 diene-phenylethene (old name acrylonitrite-butadiene-
styrene)**

The mechanism of addition polymerisation

Addition polymerisation involves free radicals in a chain
reaction. Free radicals are species which have one or
more unpaired electrons. A simple example of a free-
radical in inorganic chemistry is the chlorine atom
which has one unpaired electron. Chlorine molecules
dissociate into separate atoms in the presence of UV
light, (the explosive reaction of hydrogen with chlorine
in sunlight is a free-radical chain reaction). Addition
polymerisation takes place in three distinct stages:

- initiation
- propagation
- termination.

Initiation

To initiate the chain reaction free radicals must be
present. The source of these is an initiator. Organic
peroxides are a common initiator. They contain an O-O
bond that is easily broken by energy from heat or light.
Dibenzoyl peroxide is an example of such a peroxide.

Dibenzoyl peroxide breaks down into radicals and these
then decompose further producing phenyl radicals.

$$C_6H_5 - \overset{\overset{\displaystyle ||}{O}}{C} - O - O - \overset{\overset{\displaystyle ||}{O}}{C} - C_6H_5 \longrightarrow 2C_6H_5 - \overset{\overset{\displaystyle ||}{O}}{C} - \dot{O}$$

$$C_6H_5 - \overset{\overset{\displaystyle ||}{O}}{C} - O \longrightarrow \dot{C}_6H_5 + CO_2$$

The phenyl radical produced by the above steps is the
actual species which initiates the chain reaction.

Propagation

In the next step a phenyl radical reacts with one of the
ethene molecules by pairing its unpaired electron with
one of the electrons from the double bond. This forms
a new radical. This is called a propagation step because
a free radical is used up but another one is generated.

$$\dot{C}_6H_5 + CH_2 = CH_2 \longrightarrow C_6H_5 - CH_2 - \dot{C}H_2$$

The radical formed in this step reacts with another
ethene molecule and the chain grows.

$$C_6H_5 - CH_2 - \dot{C}H_2 + CH_2 = CH_2 \longrightarrow$$
$$C_6H_5 - CH_2 - CH_2 - CH_2 - \dot{C}H_2$$

Termination

When radicals combine they bring the chain reaction to
an end. These are called terminating steps.

$$C_6H_5 \overline{(} CH_2 \overline{)}_n \dot{C}H_2 + \dot{C}H_2 \overline{(} CH_2 \overline{)}_n C_6H_5 \longrightarrow$$
$$C_6H_5 \overline{(} CH_2 \overline{)}_n CH_2 - CH_2 \overline{(} CH_2 \overline{)}_n C_6H_5$$

9.3.2 Condensation polymerisation

Some monomers are not unsaturated. So how do they
react with one another to form a polymer? Well, this
other type of monomer consists of bifunctional
molecules. This means they have two reactive groups
(functional groups), one at each end of a short carbon
chain. Condensation polymerisation usually involves a
reaction between two different monomers, each of
which contains different functional groups. During the
reaction between the monomers, atoms from the
functional groups combine to form small molecules such
as water or hydrogen chloride. The remaining parts of
the monomers link together to form a polymer chain.
This can be represented in Box 9.7, p116.

Polyamide, PA, (nylon) is an example of a condensation
polymer. It is made commercially by reacting a dioic
acid with a diamine.

In the reaction between these monomers a hydrogen
atom from the amine group reacts with a hydroxyl
group from the acid to form water. The remaining
parts of the monomers then link together to form an
amide group.

CHEMISTRY OF POLYMERS

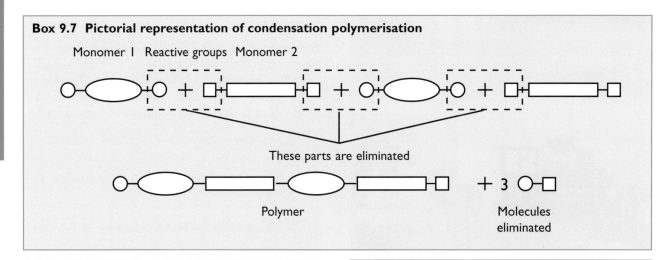

Box 9.7 Pictorial representation of condensation polymerisation

Monomer 1   Reactive groups   Monomer 2

These parts are eliminated

Polymer

+ 3

Molecules eliminated

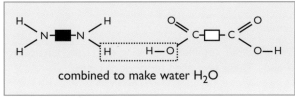

combined to make water H_2O

The resulting polymer is called a polyamide.

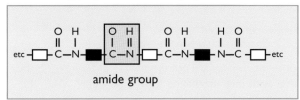

amide group

Different types of polyamide, PA, (nylon) can be made by using different monomers. If 1,6-diaminohexane is reacted with hexanedioic acid then the polymer obtained is called nylon-6,6. Using 1,6 diaminohexane with decanedioic acid produces nylon-6,10. Note that the first number refers to the number of carbon atoms in the diamine. The second number indicates the number of carbon atoms in the acid.

See Box 9.8 for the story of nylon invention.

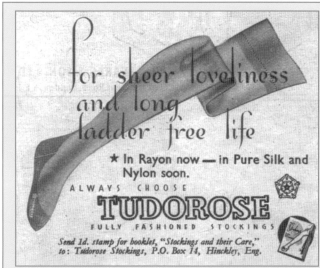

Box 9.8 The Invention of Nylon

Wallace Carothers was a chemist working for the US chemical company DuPont in the 1930's. He was working with molecules containing amine groups and carboxyl groups and was trying to make them condense to produce molecules with large rings, because compounds of this type are important in perfumery. What he actually produced were long chain molecules.

Carothers saw the potential of this. It was known that wool and silk were proteins, polymers containing ─(COHN)─ the (peptide) linkage. Carothers tried to make artificial polymers containing this linkage. He reacted diamines with dicarboxylic acids to produce polyamides, PA, (nylons).

The fibres produced in this process were rather weak. Carothers thought this was due to the water produced in the condensation process causing a hydrolysis reaction which limited the extent of polymerisation. He therefore carried out the reaction under reduced pressure. Under these conditions the water produced vaporised and the polymer produced was of better quality. The

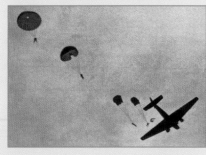

nylon produced was melted and then extruded through small holes to produce fibres. These were stretched to increase their crystalline structure and hence their strength.

DuPont commenced commercial production of the fibre in 1939 and in the Second World War nylon found a major use in the production of parachutes.

CHEMISTRY OF POLYMERS

9.4 The industrial process of Polymerisation

On an industrial scale, addition polymerisation is carried out as a large-scale process which is continuous. For a given monomer certain conditions are required to bring about polymerisation. For this reason a particular polymerisation plant will usually only be involved in making one type of plastic. Conditions in the plant determined the average molecular chain length and the degree of branching of the polymer. This is important because, as we will see (sections 9.5), these factors influence the physical properties of the polymer.

Catalysts are used for a number of reasons: to lower temperatures and pressures and to give better yields.

Catalysts can also affect the nature of the polymer produced. For example, at high temperature and pressure, ethene polymerises to produce poly(ethene), PE, with molecular chains that are not closely packed. This form of poly(ethene) is called low density poly(ethene), LDPE (see Box 9.9).

In the 1950's it was discovered that ethene could be polymerised at much lower temperatures and pressures if a special catalyst was used. It is called a Ziegler-Natta catalyst. The poly(ethene) produced is called high density poly(ethene), HDPE. The polymer chains have much less branching than is found in LDPE. This means that the chains can pack more closely together.

Finally, the solid plastic is produced as granules or a powder in order to be in a suitable form to supply to plastics processors. Chapter 8 dealt with how the plastic is processed.

Granules of amorphous PET

Box 9.9 Production of Low Density poly(ethene), LDPE

The stages in the conversion of ethene into low density poly(ethene) are:

1 Compression	The gas ethene (the monomer) is compressed to a very high pressure (2 000 - 4 000 atmospheres).
2 Reaction	The reactor is divided into three sections for preheating, reaction and after-cooling. It can be like an oven with a stirrer or it may be a long pipe which has a fluid-filled jacket which controls the temperature along its length. The conversion rate of ethene to poly(ethene) on one journey through the reactor may only be about 30%. Unreacted ethene is recycled.
3 Separation	Separation is achieved by rapidly cooling the reaction mixture so the poly(ethene) forms as a liquid and is separated from the unreacted ethene.
4 Extrusion	Extrusion is used to convert the polymer into a form suitable for transporting and then processing into useful objects. The polymer is either forced straight through a die hole and cooled so that it forms strands which are chopped up as they come out or it is allowed to solidify under water and later converted into granules. The process is a continuous one and to save energy the heat removed in the separation process is used to pre-heat the ethene prior to reaction.

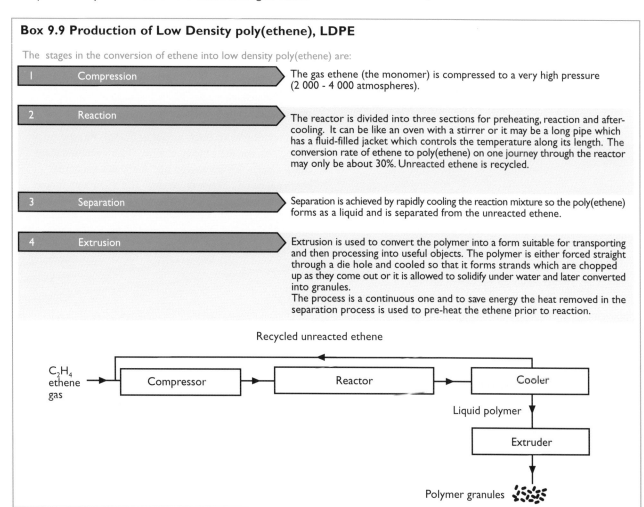

CHEMISTRY OF POLYMERS

9.5 Structure and properties

Different plastics have different physical properties. Thus, for example they differ in their strength, toughness, density, coefficient of expansion and the maximum temperature at which they can be used. They also differ in their resistance to chemicals such as acids, alkalis and organic solvents. Why should this be so? Well, not surprisingly, the answer lies in the fact that they are made of different molecules!

Within the polymer molecule the atoms are held together by strong covalent bonds. However the forces between the molecules, intermolecular forces, are relatively weak. Nevertheless it is these intermolecular forces which hold the molecules in the solid and liquid states. The size of the intermolecular forces is different for different polymers. This is why different plastics have different physical properties.

9.5.1 Intermolecular forces

To understand why the intermolecular forces are different for different plastics we need to look more closely at the nature of the covalent bonds in the plastics. Where a bond exists between atoms of two different elements, the shared electrons tend to be held closer to one of the atoms. The atom which has a greater attraction for the shared electrons is said to be more electronegative. Thus, for example, in polyesters, oxygen is more electronegative than carbon. The shared electrons are therefore displaced towards the oxygen atoms. This results in each oxygen atom having a slight negative charge. The carbon atom has a slight positive charge.

$$\overset{\delta-}{O} \\ \| \\ -\underset{\delta+}{C}-O-R$$

Ester showing bond polarity

This charge separation within a covalent bond is called a permanent dipole.

There is an attractive force between dipoles of adjacent molecules. Dipole-dipole attractions between adjacent molecules give rise to quite strong intermolecular forces. The strongest intermolecular forces are called hydrogen bonds.

Hydrogen bonds involve a particular type of permanent dipole where a highly electronegative element such as fluorine, oxygen or nitrogen is linked to a hydrogen atom. Attraction between this dipole and a second similar dipole is called hydrogen bonding. An example of this is found in polyamides. Hydrogen bonding takes place between the amine and carbonyl groups. These strong intermolecular forces account for the high melting points and the high strength of polyamides, PA,

(nylons). An example is given on page 125 of hydrogen bonding in the polyamide, Kevlar®.

In polymer molecules that contain long hydrocarbon chains, the intermolecular forces are much weaker than the dipole-dipole attractions described above. The attractive forces are due to what are called temporary dipole-induced dipole attractions.

Temporary dipoles can arise in a neutral molecule because at any one instant the electrons may not be distributed evenly between adjacent atoms. This causes small negative and positive charges to arise within the molecule and hence a temporary dipole to exist. A temporary dipole in one molecule will induce a dipole in an adjacent molecule. This is why these attractive forces are called temporary dipole-induced dipole attractions.

$$\delta+ \\ \delta- \quad \text{Molecule A}$$

$$\delta+ \\ \delta- \quad \text{Molecule B}$$

Thus, for example, a temporary dipole in A causes an induced dipole in B.

9.5.2 Intermolecular forces and physical properties

At the end of Chapter 2, thermoplastics and thermosetting plastics were introduced. How are the properties of these groups of plastic understood in terms of intermolecular forces?

In a thermoplastic, such as poly(ethene), PE, the polymer molecules consist of long chains. To a certain extent these chains are entangled but there are no actual chemical bonds between them. The attractive forces between the molecules in thermoplastics are weak.

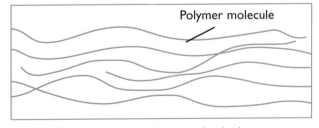

Polymer molecule

Simplified arrangement of polymer molecules in a thermoplastic

This means that thermoplastics are relatively easy to soften and melt because only a small amount of energy is needed to break the intermolecular forces and allow the polymer chains to be able to move past one another. The polymer chains themselves are unaffected by this gentle heating and when the plastic is cooled the weak intermolecular forces are sufficient to cause the plastic to once again become solid.

CHEMISTRY OF POLYMERS

Thermosetting plastics (thermosets) behave very differently when heated. They do not soften and melt when heated gently. They have a high temperature resistance but at very high temperatures they begin to char and then burn. At these high temperatures the actual structure of the polymer is broken down. This process is irreversible.

Thermosetting plastics have a different molecular structure from thermoplastics. When a thermoset is made from the monomers, polymer chains are again formed but these are linked together by strong covalent bonds. The structure is said to be highly cross-linked.

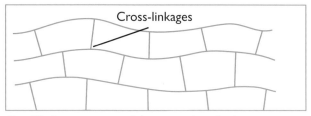

Simplified arrangement of thermosetting plastic

Because of these strong bonds throughout the thermoset, this type of plastic is rigid and cannot be melted. At high enough temperatures the covalent bonds start to break and the plastic decomposes. Hence thermosets cannot be made and then subsequently moulded into shape. They have to be moulded into shape when they are first made.

Elastomers, a subset of thermosetting plastic, have elastic or rubber-like properties. These properties can once again be accounted for in terms of molecular structure.

In thermosetting plastics, we saw that the high degree of cross-linking gives the plastic a rigid structure. In elastomers there is a limited amount of cross-linking. When the polymer is stretched the polymer chains slide past one another to a certain extent. When the tension is released, however, the cross-links between the chains ensure the plastic regains its former shape.

A representation of polymer chains in an elastomer

9.5.3 The effect of different polymer chain lengths on physical properties

The longer the molecular chains in a polymer the stronger the polymer is. To understand why this is the case, think of long pieces of string and short pieces of string. Which of these can become the most tangled and difficult to separate? Obviously, the long pieces.

The same thing is found with molecular chains. Long polymer chains become more entangled. This makes it harder for them to slide over one another and therefore the plastic is stronger. A second factor is that long chains have a greater surface area in contact with one another and this results in greater intermolecular forces.

The increase in molecular chain length required to give an increase in tensile strength is different for different polymers. Polyamide, PA, (nylon) needs an increase of about 40 repeat units but poly(ethene), PE, requires an extra 100 repeat units. This increase in length is called the critical length.

9.5.4 The effect of isomerism on physical properties

In organic chemistry isomerism is common. Isomers are compounds with the same molecular formula but the atoms are linked in different ways to one another, (see Box 9.10). The isomers have different molecular structures and these can be represented by their structural formulae.

Box 9.10 Example of isomerism

A simple example of isomerism is found in butane, C_4H_{10}. Two different structures can be drawn with this molecular formula. These two compounds differ in their properties.

$$CH_3 - CH_2 - CH_2 - CH_3 \qquad \begin{array}{c} CH_3 - CH - CH_3 \\ | \\ CH_3 \end{array}$$

Butane   **2 methylpropane**

When a polymer is made from the monomers different isomers may be produced and these isomers have different properties. This affects the use to which the plastics can be put. Thus in industrial chemistry it is important to determine the reaction conditions (temperature, pressure and nature of catalyst) that will give the best yield of the desired isomer.

Two types of isomerism are discussed in more detail below.

i. The effect of chain branching

Polymer chains are essentially linear. However, in the formation of some polymers it is possible for side chains to form.

Branched polymer molecules

CHEMISTRY OF POLYMERS

The number of side chains in a polymer has an impact on the physical properties. Straight chain isomers are able to pack more closely. These isomers, therefore, have the greater intermolecular forces since intermolecular forces are related to the area of contact possible between molecules. Thus unbranched isomers are stronger and have higher melting points and densities than their corresponding branched chain isomers.

ii. Steric structure

When a polymer is made from an unsymmetrical alkene such as propene, CH_3CHCH_2, or a substituted alkene, for example chloroethene CH_2CHCl, the substituent groups can be oriented in three different ways with respect to the carbon chain. This gives rise to three isomers which are called stereoisomers. The three stereoisomers are called isotactic, syndiotactic and atactic. These three isomers are illustrated above for poly(propene), PP.

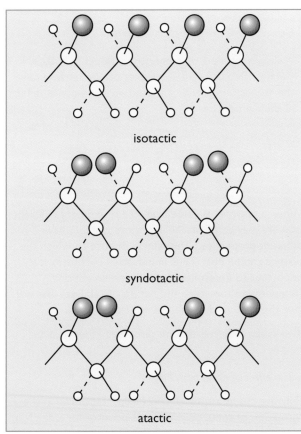

isotactic

syndotactic

atactic

The three steric structures of an unsymmetical alkene

The isotactic isomer has the most regular arrangement of CH_3 groups. The molecules are hence able to pack together more closely than in the atactic isomer. Where polymer molecules are able to pack together closely the structure is described as being crystalline. The atactic isomer does not have the molecules packed closely together. It is not crystalline but is described as amorphous.

The degree of crystallinity of a polymer affects its physical properties. This is discussed in the next section.

9.5.5 Crystallinity of polymers

Crystals, of course, are regular flat-sided solids in which the molecules are arranged in an ordered fashion. Now in polymer chemistry the term is used with a slightly different meaning. Polymer chains that are closely packed have a molecular structure which has order and are described as being crystalline (even though actual crystals are not formed). Polymers in which the chains are not closely packed and are arranged randomly are said to be amorphous. Often a plastic will contain both crystalline and amorphous regions.

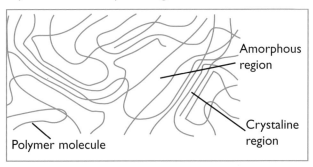

Amorphous region

Crystaline region

Polymer molecule

Regions in thermoplastic

As we have seen the crystallinity of a polymer is affected by whether the molecules are linear or branched and also by whether the linear chain is isotactic or atactic. The degree of crystallinity influences the physical properties of the plastic. Highly crystalline polymers have a higher density and softening temperature than amorphous polymers. Highly crystalline polymers are also less flexible and have a lower transparency than amorphous polymers.

9.5.6 Changes of state and transitions

When a pure substance consisting of simple molecules is heated it melts and eventually boils. With polymers the situation is more complicated.

At a low enough temperature all plastics are rigid and glassy in nature. Intermolecular forces are sufficient to prevent any movement of molecular chains with respect to one another.

For thermoplastics, as the temperature is raised, a point is reached above which the polymer becomes flexible and can be moulded. At this point the polymer chains can move relative to one another and are rotating about their backbone ('crankshaft motion'). This transition temperature is called the glass transition temperature, Tg.

At a sufficiently high temperature, the melting point, there is enough thermal energy to overcome intermolecular forces and allow the molecules to move past one another. The plastic is then a viscous fluid.

CHEMISTRY OF POLYMERS

| Rigid and glassy solid | Heat (Tg) ⇌ Cool | Flexible and plastic solid | Heat (Tm) → ⇌ Cool | Viscous fluid |

Thermosetting plastics are destroyed at high temperatures.

9.6 Additives and the formulation of plastics

The former sections have shown how the physical properties of a plastic relate to the molecular structure of the polymer. In addition, the properties can be modified to suit the needs of particular applications by using various additives (see Box 9.11).

A good example of this is poly(chloroethene), PVC. Advertisements describe window frames, gutters and piping as made from uPVC. What does the 'u' mean? uPVC is unplasticised PVC. This type of PVC is rigid and hard and these properties are required for the applications given.

Plasticisers are a particular type of additive. When added to a polymer they act as a molecular lubricant. The molecules of plasticiser get in-between the polymer chains and allow the chains to slide over one another more easily.

When PVC is mixed with plasticisers the product is very flexible and can be used to make articles such as shower curtains and plastic tubing. The addition of plasticisers to a polymer lowers the glass transition temperature, Tg, value of a plastic. This means that the plastic can be shaped at a lower temperature.

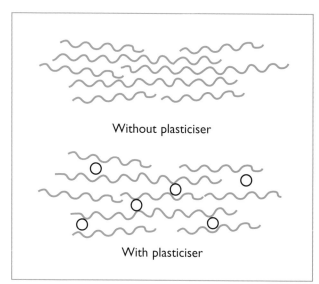

Without plasticiser

With plasticiser

Box 9.11 Functions of additives	
Function	**Additives**
Extend working life	• antioxidants to prevent reaction with oxygen • light stabilisers to prevent colours from fading • stabilisers to inhibit undesirable degradation in use • absorbers to protect against harmful effects of UV light • flame retardants to help prevent ignition or spread of flame
Improve working properties	• fibres to improve mechanical strength • antistatic agents to prevent build up of dust through static • impact modifiers to help plastic mouldings absorb shock
Assist processing	• waxes and lubricants as heat stabilisers to prevent decomposition during processing • plasticisers to make plastics softer and easier to mould • blowing agents to produce foamed materials • compatibilisers to blend different waste plastics for recycling
Enhance appearance	• pigments for colour
Reduce costs	• fillers such as talc or powdered minerals

CHEMISTRY OF POLYMERS

9.7 Summary of polymer classification

Polymers can be classified in a variety of ways and these are summarised in Box 9.12 below.

Box 9.12 Classification of polymers

Classification		Notes
Thermoplastics	Effect of heat	Soften when heated and harden on cooling. Cycle can be repeated over and over again without chemical change. Linear or branched chain structure without cross links between the chains.
Thermosets		Cannot be resoftened by heating. Extensive three-dimensional cross-linking occurs to give permanently hard materials.
Addition	Method of polymerisation	Usually from monomers containing a –CH=CH– unit. Involves initiation, propagation and termination reactions. Initiation may be by (1) free radical e.g. in the production of poly(chloroethene), PVC, poly(phenylethene), PS, low density poly(ethene), phenylethene/buta-1,3-diene rubber and poly(methyl-2-methylpropenoate), PMMA. (2) protonation by a Lewis acid (cationic) e.g. in butyl rubber production. (3) carbanion formation e.g. in poly(buta-1,3-diene) production. (4) coordination complex formation to give a linear highly stereospecific product e.g. in high density poly(ethene), HDPE and poly(propene), PP production.
Condensation		Generally gives different alternating structural units from condensation reactions between different molecules. Nylon-6,6, polyesters, and phenolic, urea and methanal resins are examples, as also are the silicone rubbers.
Elastomers	Modulus of elasticity (for linear polymers)	Low. Rubber, polychloroprene.
Plastics		Medium. Poly(chloroethene), PVC, poly(ethenyl ethanoate),
Fibres		High. Polyamides, PA, silk, polyesters, cellulose.
Homopolymer	Formula	Contain one monomer unit, e.g. poly(ethene), PE poly(chloroethene), PVC.
Copolymer		Block alternating or random arrangement of two or more monomers. Or side-chains may be of one monomer, the main chain another (graft).
Linear	Chemical structure	Linear chains may take up straight, zig-zag, coiled or random spatial arrangements.
Branched		Long or short branched chains attached to main chain.
Cross-linked		Two- or three-dimensionsal cross-linking between chains.
Isotactic	Steric structure Such polymers are produced by Ziegler-Natta catalyst systems which give stereospecific orientation of polymers.	All side groups are on same side of chain.
Syndiotactic		Each alternate side group has same orientation.
Atactic		No specific orientation of side groups – randomly arranged.

APPENDIX

The appendix gives some brief descriptions of the chemistry to produce plastics found in the post-16 curriculum.

1. CELLULOSE ETHANOATE (ACETATE)

Cellulose ethanoate is a semi-synthetic plastic in that it is made by chemically modifying the natural polymer cellulose. It is used to make film for wrapping, particularly for flowers.

Cellulose consists of a three-dimensional network of chains of glucose units. The structure of a glucose unit is:

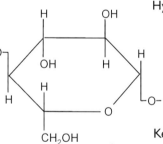

The structure of cellulose is:

Cellulose ethanoate is made by ethanoylating (acetylating) cellulose with ethanoic anhydride. This esterifies one hydroxyl group per molecule if the appropriate amount of ethanoic anhydride is used.

$$X\text{-}OH + (CH_3CO)_2O \longrightarrow X\text{-}O\text{-}CO\text{-}CH_3 + CH_3COOH$$

cellulose   ethanoic anhydride   cellulose ethanoate   ethanoic acid

A greater proportion of the anhydride leads to the formation of the diethanoate and then the triethanoate. The latter is used as a synthetic fibre called Tricel.

2. KEVLAR®

Kevlar® is a polyamide like nylon. It is, however, a polyamide with a difference!

Following the invention of nylon, chemists developed a better understanding of the relationship between the structure of a polymer and its properties such as strength. At the beginning of the 1960s, the chemical company DuPont decided to try and develop a fibre that had the heat resistance of asbestos and the stiffness of glass.

The nylon family of polymers are already quite strong. How could they be made stronger? The DuPont chemists decided to investigate the properties of aromatic polyamides. These contain a benzene ring which gives the polymer chain more rigidity than an aliphatic chain. Thus, Kevlar® is particularly strong because the polymer chains are rigid and linear. Hydrogen bonds hold the chains together forming sheets of molecules. The sheets then stack together in a regular fashion around the fibre axis giving a highly ordered structure. Kevlar® adopts this structure because of the way the polymer is processed to produce the fibre.

Kevlar®

Kevlar® is a 'super fibre'. It is fire resistant, flexible and very strong. Mass for mass, Kevlar® is about five times stronger than steel. Many uses have been developed for this remarkable fibre including replacing steel cords in tyres, making bullet-proof vests, strengthening the rigging of yachts and frames of tennis raquets. A stiffer form of Kevlar® is used in making aircraft wings.

Structure of Kevlar®

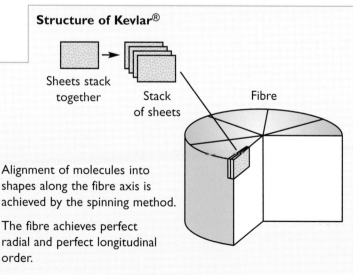

Sheets stack together   Stack of sheets   Fibre

Alignment of molecules into shapes along the fibre axis is achieved by the spinning method.

The fibre achieves perfect radial and perfect longitudinal order.

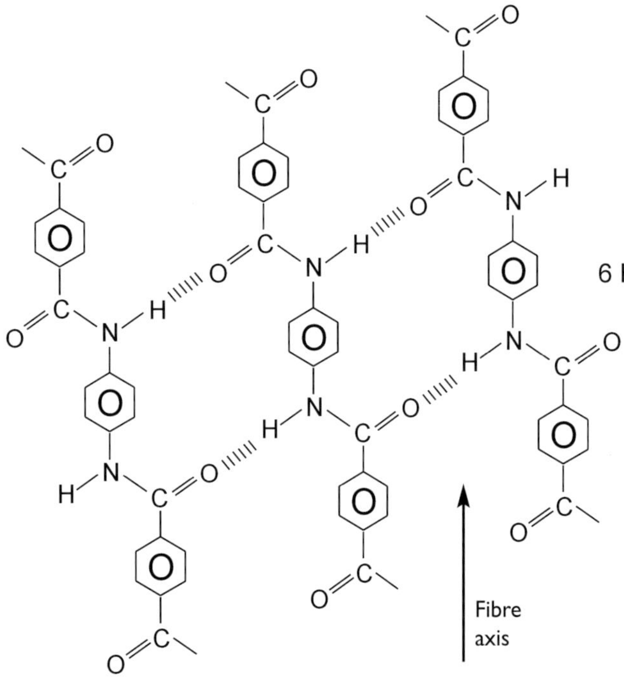

Fibre axis

The monomers

Kevlar® is made from two monomers which are both readily available and quite cheap. The monomers are 1,4-benzene dioylchloride and 1,4-diaminobenzene.

1,4-benzenedioyl chloride

1,4-diaminobenzene

The 1,4-benzenedioyl chloride is made from benzene 1,4-dicarboxylic acid.

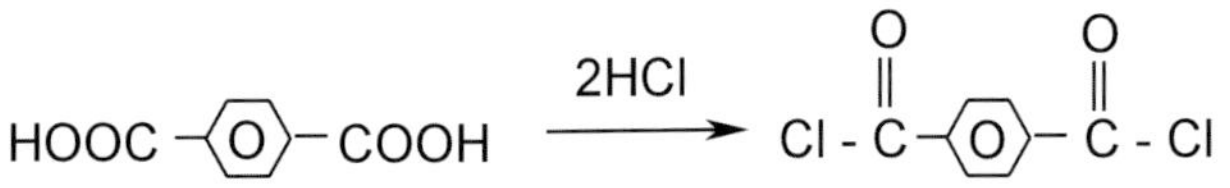

1,4 benzenedioyl chloride

The Polymerisation

The monomers are reacted together in a condensation reaction. The only suitable solvent for the reaction was found to be concentrated sulphuric acid. The Kevlar® is precipitated from the solution at the end of the reaction.

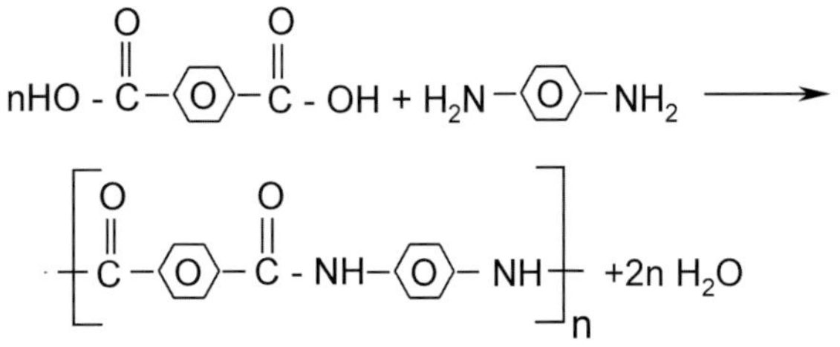

3. MELAMINE-METHANAL PLASTICS

Melamine resins are colourless and resistant to heat, light and moisture. They are used to make light-weight picnic and tableware. Kitchen worktops have a cheaper phenolic resin as the base and are then coated with a more expensive melamine surface.

Manufacture of the monomers

Methanal (see Phenol-methanal plastics)

Melamine is made by heating carbamide (urea).

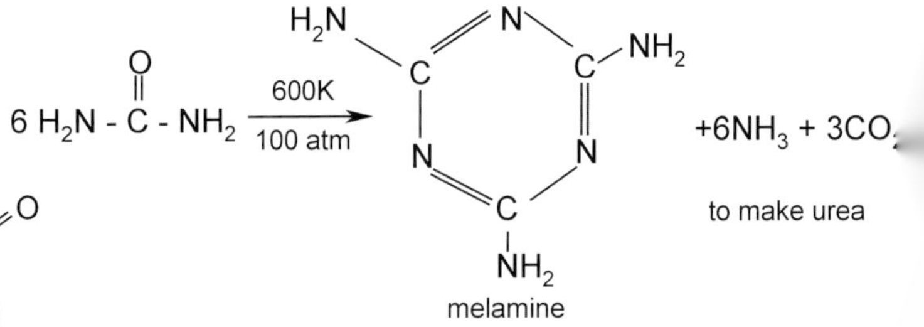

$6 H_2N - C - NH_2 \xrightarrow[100 \ atm]{600K}$ +6NH_3 + 3CO_2

to make urea

melamine

Manufacture of the polymer

Melamine is reacted with methanal in alkaline solution:

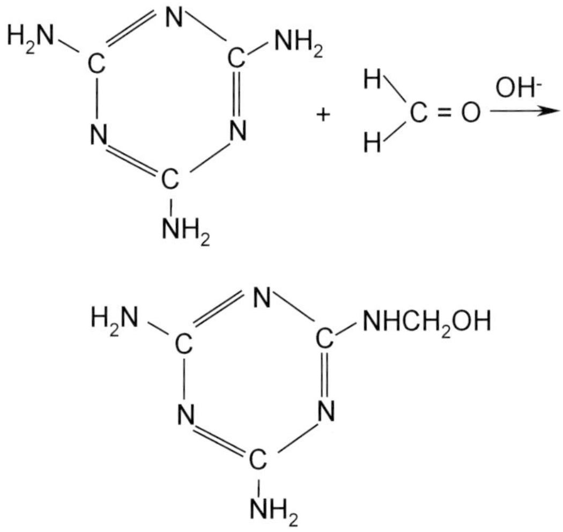

The products condense in acid conditions, eliminating water and forming a linear polymer with a structure analogous to that for carbamide-methanal polymers.

Upon further heating more condensation reactions occur producing a cross-linked structure.

4. PHENOL-METHANAL PLASTICS (BAKELITE)

Bakelite is one of the oldest plastics; Baekland patented the process in 1910.

Bakelite, a thermoset, has a giant 3-dimensional cross-linked structure similar to that of diamond, resulting in resistance to high temperatures but at very high temperatures the structure of the polymer breaks down and it chars.

The high degree of cross-linking within the structure, together with the strength of the bonds, makes Bakelite generally unreactive and very insoluble. The polymer is also a very good electrical insulator. Major uses include making worktops, printed circuit boards and electrical fittings.

Manufacture of the monomers

Phenol is made from benzene. Firstly this is converted to 1-methylethylbenzene (cumene).

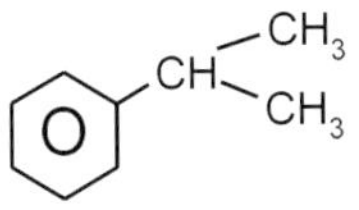

This is then oxidised with air to form a hydroperoxide which is then decomposed using warm, dilute sulphuric acid to produce phenol and propanone.

Methanal is prepared from methane in a series of stages; starting from methane.

$$CH_{4(g)} + H_2O_{(g)} \xrightarrow[\text{1178K 30 atm}]{\text{Ni catalyst}} CO_{(g)} + 3H_{2(g)}$$

$$CO_{(g)} + 2H_{2(g)} \xrightarrow[\text{570K, 300 atm}]{\text{ZnO, Cr}_2O_3} CH_3OH_{(g)}$$

$$CH_3OH_{(g)} + \tfrac{1}{2}O_{2(g)} \xrightarrow[\text{770K}]{\text{Ag catalyst}}$$

Manufacture of the polymer

Phenol reacts with methanal when heated in sodium hydroxide solution. The reaction takes place in two stages:

i. Forming the polymer chain

Phenol undergoes a substitution reaction, in the 2- or 4-position, with methanal.

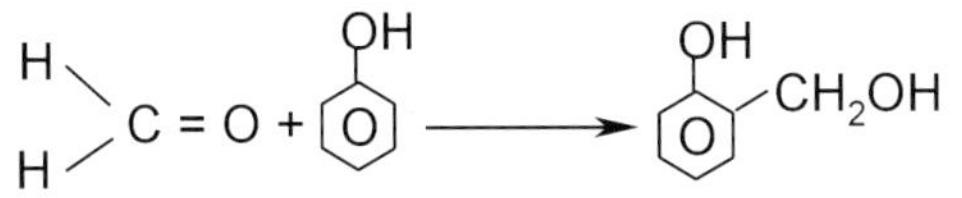

The product then undergoes a condensation reaction with another molecule of phenol, with the elimination of a molecule of water.

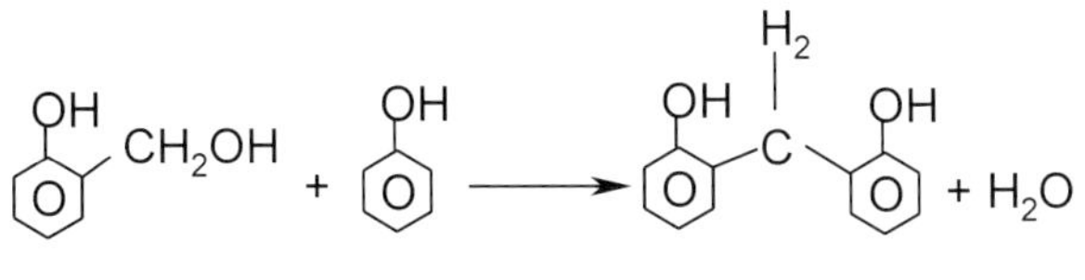

Further condensation reactions take place as methanal and phenol react alternately with the product. This builds up a polymer chain.

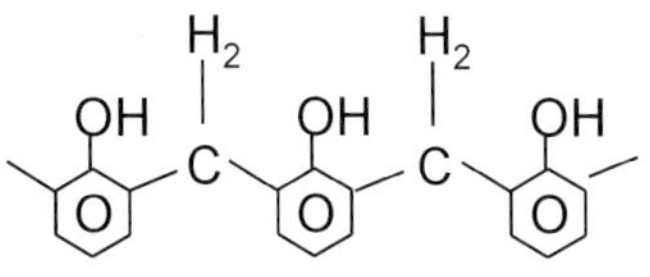

a 'resole' resin

ii. Forming covalent cross-links between the chains

In this stage the benzene ring in phenol reacts at other positions. A 3-dimensional cross-linked structure is formed.

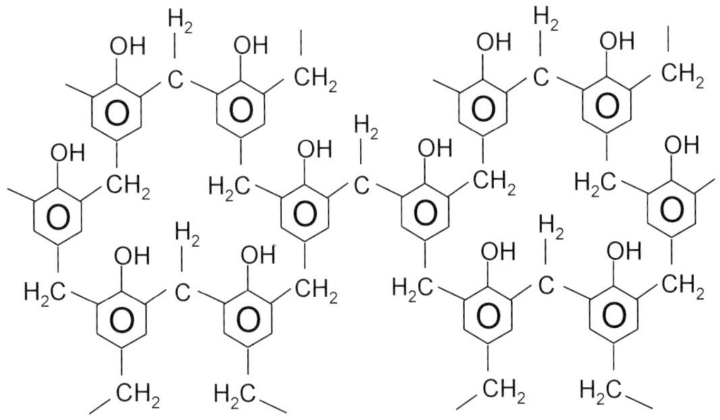

Diagram of 3-D structure

5. POLY(CARBONATES), PC

Manufacture of the monomers

Bisphenol A is made by condensing phenol with propanone:

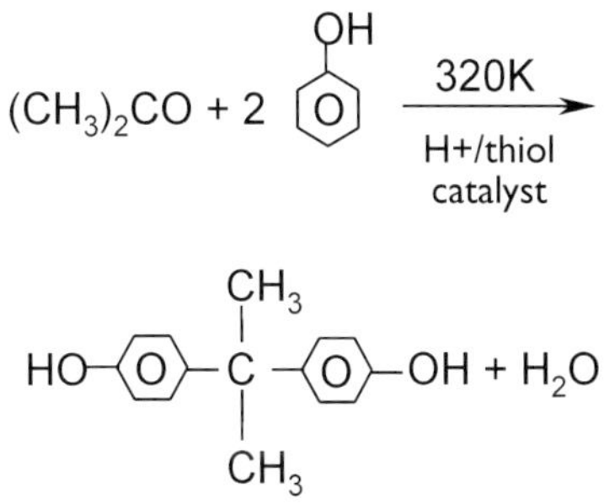

bisphenol A

The other monomer is carbonyl chloride. This is made by reacting carbon monoxide with chlorine.

$$CO_{(g)} + Cl_{2(g)} \longrightarrow COCl_{2(g)}$$

Manufacture of the polymer

Bisphenol A is reacted with carbonyl chloride in a basic solution of pyridine in dichloromethane:

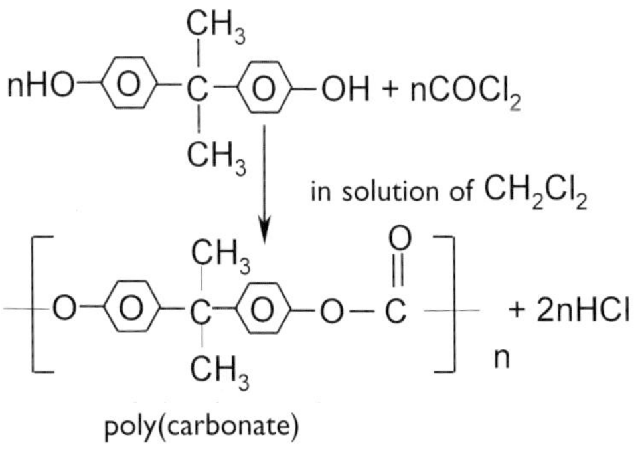

poly(carbonate)

6. POLY(CHLOROETHENE), PVC

PVC is a very versatile plastic which can be plasticised to give a product with variable properties over the complete range of flexibility from rigid to pliable.

Manufacture of the monomer

Ethene is reacted with chlorine to produce dichloroethane:

$$CH_2 = CH_2 + Cl_2 \xrightarrow{FeCl_3} ClCH_2CH_2Cl$$

Dichloroethane can also be made by reacting ethene with hydrogen chloride and oxygen (in air) using a catalyst of copper(II) chloride and potassium chloride.

$$CH_2 = CH_2 + 2HCl + \tfrac{1}{2} O_2 \longrightarrow ClCH_2CH_2Cl + H_2O$$

The 1,2-dichloroethane is then heated (cracked) which causes the elimination of hydrogen chloride, forming chloroethene.

$$ClCH_2 - CH_2 - Cl \xrightarrow{heat} CH_2 = CH - Cl + HCl$$
chloroethene

Manufacture of the polymer

Chloroethene is polymerised in a free-radical reaction. In the commonest process, the monomer is dispersed in water and polymerisation is carried out at 13 atm. pressure and a temperature of 325 - 350K. The initiator is an organic peroxide.

$$n\ CH_2 = CHCl \longrightarrow \left[CH_2 - CHCl \right]_n$$

chloroethene   poly(chloroethene)

7. POLYESTERS

Granules of the PET can be melted and squeezed through fine holes to produce filaments. These can then be used to make fibre. PET can also be used to make film. In the most recently developed use polyester granules are heated to bring about further polymerisation. The polymer is then stretched and moulded, into bottles for example. The arrangement of the polymer chains is different in the fibres, the film and the bottles.

In fibres, the molecules are mainly arranged in one direction (a), in film, they are in two directions (b) and for packaging, they are in three directions (c).

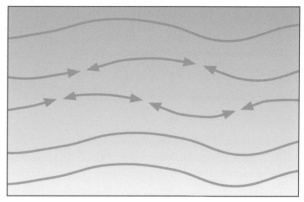

(a) Fibres: the molecules are mostly in one direction (Terylene and Dacron)

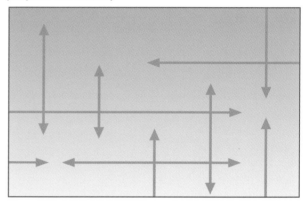

(b) Film: the molecules are in two directions

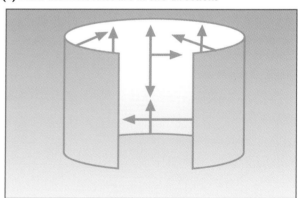

(c) For bottles: the polymer molecules are arranged in three directions

Manufacture of the monomers

Benzene 1,4-dicarboxylic acid is made by oxidising 1,4-dimethylbenzene. Air is passed into the liquid under pressure at about 400K. A cobalt salt is used as a catalyst.

$$\underset{CH_3}{\overset{CH_3}{\bigcirc}} + 3O_2 \longrightarrow \underset{CO_2H}{\overset{CO_2H}{\bigcirc}} + 2H_2O$$

Ethanediol is prepared by oxidising ethene to epoxyethane. This is then reacted with water.

$$CH_2 = CH_2 + \tfrac{1}{2}O_2 \xrightarrow[\text{550 K}]{\text{Ag catalyst}} H_2C \underset{O}{\overset{\diagdown \diagup}{-}} CH_2$$

ethene   epoxyethane

$$H_2C \underset{O}{\overset{\diagdown \diagup}{-}} CH_2 + H_2O \xrightarrow[\text{350 K, pressure}]{\text{acid solution}}$$

$$H\,O - CH_2 - CH_2 - OH$$

ethene-1,2-diol

Manufacture of the polymer

Benzene 1,4-dicarboxylic acid is reacted with ethanediol to produce a diester which is referred to as the PET monomer. Some low molecular mass oligomers are produced containing up to 5 monomer units.

$$HO - \overset{O}{\overset{\|}{C}} - \langle O \rangle - \overset{O}{\overset{\|}{C}} - OH + 2HO - CH_2 - CH_2 - OH$$

autocatalysed by -COOH group

$$HO - CH_2 - CH_2 - O - \overset{O}{\overset{\|}{C}} - \langle O \rangle - \overset{O}{\overset{\|}{C}} - O - CH_2 - CH_2 - OH + 2H_2O$$

The PET monomer is then heated to 535-575K with a catalyst of antimony(III)oxide. Further condensation then occurs with the elimination of ethane1,2-diol.

$$nHO - CH_2 - CH_2 - O - \overset{O}{\overset{\|}{C}} - \langle O \rangle - \overset{O}{\overset{\|}{C}} - O - CH_2 - CH_2 - OH$$

$$\longrightarrow \left[\overset{O}{\overset{\|}{C}} - \langle O \rangle - \overset{O}{\overset{\|}{C}} - O - CH_2 - CH_2 - O \right]_n$$

$$+ \ n \ HOCH_2CH_2OH$$

8. POLY(ETHENE), PE

There are three forms of poly(ethene): low density, LDPE, linear low density, LLDPE and high density, HDPE. LDPE and LLDPE are used for film packaging and electrical insulation. HDPE is used to make containers for household chemicals and plastic drums for industry. These are made by blow moulding. All forms of poly(ethene) can be used for injection-moulded products including buckets, washing-up bowls and food boxes.

Manufacture of the monomer

Ethene is made by cracking naphtha.

Manufacture of LDPE

Ethene is polymerised at about 420 - 570K using high pressures of 1000 - 3000 atm. Oxygen and/or an organic peroxide is used as the initiator.

$$n \ H_2C = CH_2 \longrightarrow \left[CH_2 - CH_2 \right]_n$$

The polymer chains produced contain short branches (about 20 branches per 1000 carbon atoms). These reduce the crystallinity and density of the polymer.

Manufacture of HDPE

Ethene is polymerised in an inert solvent (for example, hexane) containing a suspension of a Ziegler-Natta catalyst. A temperature of 310 - 360K is used and pressures of 1 - 50 atm. Linear polymer chains are produced with few branches. The chains therefore can pack more closely than in low density poly(ethene), LDPE, giving a product which is more crystalline, denser, stronger and more rigid than LDPE.

Manufacture of LLDPE

LDPE has many uses but the manufacturing process requires high pressure resulting in high capital costs of equipment. A low density form of poly(ethene), PE called linear low density poly(ethene), LLDPE can be made by a process similar to that used to make high density poly(ethene), HDPE, however, small amounts of but-1-ene or hex-1-ene are added as a co-polymer to reduce the density of the HDPE polymer. The co-polymers produce short chain branches along the carbon chain. The product has good resilience, tear strength and flexibility without the use of plasticisers. It is ideal for making film products such as wrappings.

9. POLY(METHYL 2-METHYLPROPENOATE), PMMA,

Manufacture of the monomer

The monomer is methyl 2-methylpropenoate:

$$\overset{\overset{\displaystyle CH_3}{\displaystyle |}}{H_2C = C} - CO_2CH_3$$

This is made in steps from propanone. First an addition compound is made by reaction with hydrogen cyanide.

$$CH_3COCH_3 + HCN \longrightarrow \overset{\overset{\displaystyle CN}{\displaystyle |}}{CH_3 - C - CH_3} \underset{\displaystyle |}{} \\ OH$$

This is dehydrated using concentrated sulphuric acid which also hydrolyses the nitrile group to an amide.

$$\underset{\overset{|}{\underset{OH}{CH_3 - C - CH_3}}}{\overset{CN}{|}} \longrightarrow \underset{\overset{|}{CH_3}}{\overset{CN}{H_2C = C - CH_3}} \longrightarrow \underset{\overset{|}{CH_3}}{\overset{CONH_2}{H_2C = C - CH_3}}$$

The amide is then reacted with methanol to produce the monomer.

$$\underset{\overset{|}{CH_3}}{\overset{CONH_2}{H_2C = C - CH_3}} \longrightarrow \underset{\overset{|}{CH_3}}{\overset{CO_2H}{H_2C = C - CH_3}} \longrightarrow \underset{\overset{|}{CH_3}}{\overset{CO_2CH_3}{H_2C = C - CH_3}}$$

Manufacture of the polymer

This is brought about using a free radical initiator such as a peroxide.

$$n \ \underset{\overset{|}{CO_2CH_3}}{\overset{CH_3}{H_2C = C}} \longrightarrow \left[\underset{\overset{|}{CO_2CH_3}}{\overset{CH_3}{H_2C - C}} \right]_n$$

A small amount of a co-monomer such as ethyl propenoate is often added. This decreases the viscosity of the molten polymer and also gives increased thermal stability.

10. POLY(PHENYLETHENE) or POLY(STYRENE), PS

Manufacture of phenylethene

Benzene is first converted to ethylbenzene by reacting it with ethene in the presence of an aluminium chloride catalyst:

$$\langle O \rangle + H_2C = CH_2 \xrightarrow[600K, \ 40 \ atm]{AlCl_3 \ catalyst} \langle O \rangle - CH_2 - CH_3$$

Ethylbenzene is then dehydrogenated by passing it over a heated catalyst of iron(III) oxide.

$$\langle O \rangle - CH_2 - CH_3 \xrightarrow[900K]{Fe_2O_3 \ catalyst} \langle O \rangle - CH = CH_2 + H_2$$

Polymerisation of phenylethene

Phenylethene is polymerised in a free-radical reaction which may be carried out in the bulk monomer or in aqueous suspension using an organic peroxide initiator.

$$n \ \underset{\overset{|}{CH_2}}{\overset{C_6H_5}{HC = CH_2}} \longrightarrow \left[\underset{\overset{|}{CH - CH_2}}{\overset{C_6H_5}{}} \right]_n$$

To make expanded poly(phenylethene) the polymer is manufactured in the form of beads containing pentane. This vaporises when heated and the beads expand. The beads are then blown into moulds and fused together by further heating.

11. POLY(PROPENE), PP

Poly(propene), PP is a versatile thermoplastic. It can be made into film for packaging and into fibres for clothing and carpets. It can also be used in injection moulding to produce articles such as washing-up bowls and car bumpers. Additives can be used to produce materials that are suited to an even wider range of applications.

Most poly(propene), PP is produced as the homopolymer, that is, propene is the only monomer. Some PP is made in the form of a co-polymer with ethene. The presence of the ethene reduces the crystallinity and melting point of the polymer. The flexibility is also greater and the product is more translucent. The ethene units may either be introduced randomly into the polymer chains or may be incorporated as a block. In this second type of co-polymer propene is initially polymerised to give a homopolymer. Then in a second stage propene and ethene are co-polymerised to produce what is called a block co-polymer.

Manufacture of the polymer

Propene is polymerised using Ziegler-Natta catalysts.

There are two processes used:

$$n \ \underset{\overset{|}{CH + CH_2}}{\overset{CH_3}{}} \longrightarrow \left[\underset{\overset{|}{CH - CH_2}}{\overset{CH_3}{}} \right]_n$$

i. The Bulk Process

Liquid propene is polymerised at 320 - 360 K and with a pressure of 20 - 40 atm.

ii. The Gas Phase Process

Gaseous propene fluidises particles of solid catalyst. A temperature of 320 - 360 K is used with a pressure of 8 - 35 atm. If two reactors are used in series then block co-polymers can be produced.

12. POLY(TETRAFLUOROETHENE), PTFE

PTFE contains very strong C-F bonds. These make the polymer very stable and unreactive. PTFE is very resistant to attack by chemicals, is an excellent electrical insulator and has very low friction, non-stick properties.

$$CH_4 + 3Cl_2 \longrightarrow CHCl_3 + 3HCl$$

Manufacture of the monomer, TFE

Methane is converted to trichloromethane by reaction with a mixture of chlorine and hydrochloric acid. This can be brought about in the liquid phase at 370 - 420 K using a zinc chloride catalyst. The reaction can also be carried out in the vapour phase using a different catalyst and temperature.

$$CHCl_3 + 2HF \longrightarrow CHClF_2 + 2HCl$$

The trichloromethane is then converted to chlorodifluoromethane by reaction with anhydrous hydrogen fluoride in the presence of antimony(III) chloride:

$$2CHClF_2 \rightleftharpoons CF_2 = CF_2 + 2HCl$$

The chlorodifluoromethane is then cracked at atmospheric pressure and temperatures of 940 - 1070K to form TFE. TFE is a highly unstable gas and, once formed, has to be cooled rapidly to prevent its explosive decomposition.

Manufacture of the polymer

Since TFE is so unstable it is converted quickly to the polymer to minimise storage time. TFE is passed into water at 310 - 350K and a pressure of 10 - 20 atm. A radical initiator such as ammonium persulphate is used.

$$n\ CF_2 = CF_2 \longrightarrow \left[CF_2 - CF_2 \right]_n$$

TFE   PTFE

13. POLYURETHANES, PU

The polyurethanes, PU are a family of addition polymers whose physical properties depend on the identity of the original reactants. The polyurethanes are different from other addition polymers in that there is no urethane monomer. They are usually made directly into the desired product, that is the chemical reaction which produces a polyurethane takes place in the mould itself.

Polyurethanes, PU are made by reacting an alcohol with two or more hydroxyl groups (-OH) with an isocyanate containing more than one isocyanate group (-NCO) per molecule.

Manufacture of the reactants

i. Manufacture of isocyanates

There are two isocyanates of particular importance. These are TDI (toluene diisocyanate) and MDI (diisocyanate-diphenylmethane). The production of TDI is described below.

TDI is actually a mixture of diisocyanates.

Firstly methylbenzene (toluene) is nitrated to produce two isomers of nitromethylbenzene (NMB):

2-NMB   4-NMB

These are then nitrated further, producing a mixture of dinitromethylbenzenes. The trivial names for these are still used in industry. They are 2,4-dinitrotoluene and 2,6-dinitrotoluene (DNT).

2,4 DNT   2,6 DNT

The isomers of DNT are then reduced, forming the corresponding amines:

These are then reacted with carbonyl chloride to produce the diisocyanates:

ii. Manufacture of Polyols

These are common industrial chemicals. The polyol used has a significant effect on the properties of the polymer. The number of hydroxyl groups per molecule and the size and flexibility of the molecular structure affects the degree of cross-linking and hence the rigidity of the polymer.

Manufacture of the polymer

The liquid reactants are mixed. The reaction starts immediately and is complete within about 1 minute.

$$n \; O = C = N - R' - N = C = O +$$

di-isocyanate

$$n \; HO - R - OH \longrightarrow$$

diol

polyurethane

14. SILICONE RUBBERS

Silicone rubbers are non-organic, synthetic elastomers. Silicones are polymers whose backbone consists of alternating silicon and oxygen atoms. Alkyl or aryl groups are attached to the silicon atoms.

Silicones are classified into three groups - fluids, rubbers and resins, depending upon their physical properties. These, in turn, are determined by the molecular structure of the polymer. In silicone rubbers a limited degree of cross-linking is introduced between the chains. This results in a structure similar to natural rubber and the polymer is an elastomer.

Silicone rubbers are not as strong as natural rubber at ordinary temperatures, but they are more stable at low temperatures (200K) and at high temperatures (450 - 600K). Silicone rubbers are generally more resistant to chemical attack, however, and have a good resistance to ageing.

Manufacture of the monomers

Pure silicon is made by reducing silicon dioxide with carbon at high temperatures.

$$SiO_2 + 2C \longrightarrow Si + 2CO$$

The silicon is then converted into chlorosilanes. For example, if chloromethane is passed through heated silicon at 550 - 600K under slight pressure, a mixture of chlorosilanes is produced which can be purified by fractionation. The main product is dimethyldichlorosilane, with some of the methyl and trimethyl derivatives also being formed.

$$Si + 2CH_3Cl \xrightarrow{500 - 600K} (CH_3)_2 \; SiCl_2$$

dimethyldichlorosilane

Manufacture of the polymer

The dichlorosilanes are hydrolysed forming dialkylsilanediols $R_2Si(OH)_2$. These polymerise spontaneously forming long linear chains.

The extent of polymerisation is controlled by the use of a certain amount of the trialkylmonochlorosilane. This molecule is called an 'end blocker'.

In making silicon rubbers only a very small amount of end blocker is used. The reactant is, for example, 99.9% dimethyldichlorosilane. Silicone rubbers have a little cross-linking.

15. VISCOSE RAYON

Cellulosic fibres were first produced on a commercial scale in France in 1891. The fibre was known as Chardonnet silk or rayon. The fabric looks and feels like silk but is not as light or strong. Rayon is not a plastic. It is, however, a man-made fibre and the first one to be produced commercially. Rayon is mainly used in the clothing industry.

Viscose rayon is now made by a different process from the original Chardonnet method. Cellulose is reacted with sodium hydroxide and carbon disulphide to produce a solution of cellulose xanthate.

cellulose   cellulose xanthate

When this solution is squirted through fine jets into a solution of sulphuric acid fine fibres of cellulose are precipitated out of solution. These fibres are called viscose rayon.

132

Names and structures of commodity polymers and their monomers *(Traditional names are given in italics)*

systematic name of monomer(s)	structure of monomer(s)	systematic name of polymer	structure of polymer	abbreviation	example of trade names
ethene *ethylene*	$CH_2{=}CH_2$	low density poly(ethene) *low density polyethylene*	$\left[CH_2\text{-}CH_2\right]_n$	LDPE	Lacqtene*
ethene *ethylene*	$CH_2{=}CH_2$	high density poly(ethene) *high density polyethylene*	$\left[CH_2\text{-}CH_2\right]_n$	HDPE	Lacqtene* Finathene Finacene
propene *propylene*	$CH_2{=}CH\text{-}CH_3$	poly(propene) *polypropylene*	$\left[CH_2\text{-}\underset{\underset{CH_3}{\mid}}{CH}\right]_n$	PP	Atofina, PP
ethane-1,2-diol *ethylene glycol* benzene-1,4-dicarboxylic acid *terephthalic acid*	$HO\text{-}CH_2\text{-}CH_2\text{-}OH$ $HOOC\text{-}C_6H_4\text{-}COOH$	poly(oxy-1,2-ethanediyl oxycarbonyl-1,4-phenylene carbonyl) *polyethylene terephthalate*	$\left[\overset{O}{\overset{\|}{C}}\text{-}C_6H_4\text{-}\overset{O}{\overset{\|}{C}}\text{-}O\text{-}(CH_2)_2\text{-}O\right]_n$	PET	Tergal
phenylethene *styrene*	$CH_2{=}CH\text{-}C_6H_5$	poly(phenylethene) *polystyrene*	$\left[CH_2\text{-}\underset{\underset{C_6H_5}{\mid}}{CH}\right]_n$	PS	Lacqrene*
chloroethene *chloroethylene or vinyl chloride*	$CH_2{=}CH\text{-}Cl$	poly(chloroethene) *polyvinyl chloride*	$\left[CH_2\text{-}\underset{\underset{Cl}{\mid}}{CH}\right]_n$	PVC	Lacovyl*

* The discovery of Elf's first gas field in 1951 at Lacq, in the French Pyrenees, resulted in the production of these polymers. This history is reflected in their names *Lacq*tene and *Lac*ovyl.

*the table below lists the various polymers discussed in this booklet, in addition to commodity polymers.

Other polymers*		
abbreviation	names (systematic name - normal type, traditional names - *italic*), structures and comments	example of trade names
styrenics	*acrylonitrile/butadiene/styrene* (a co-polymer of the three monomers below). The abbreviation ABS is formed from the initial letters of the old name of the monomers. propenonitrile/buta-1,3-diene/phenylethene is the systematic name *styrene/butadiene/styrene co-polymer*	ABS Finaprene Finaclear
epoxy	polyepoxides: polymers containing the structure (produced from addition of an epoxy function to an alcohol function)	Araldite
EPS	expanded *polystyrene* or expanded phenylethene, EPS contains a blowing agent which produces a gas and expands the molten PS at around $220°C$	
EVA	*poly(ethylene/vinyl acetate)* also known as poly(ethylene/ethenyl ethanoate) a co-polymer of these two monomers: 	Evatane
EVOH	*poly(vinyl alcohol)* also known as poly(ethenol) is made from the monomer	Soarnol
PA	polyamides polymers containing the structures $-CH_2-$ and $-O-\overset{O}{\overset{\|}{C}}-NH-$ example: polyamide 11 [PA 11] or nylon 11 other common PAs: PA 6 or nylon 6, PA 6,6 or nylon 6,6, PA 12 or nylon 12	Nylon Rilsan
PBT	*polybutylene terephthalate* a polymer of *butanediol* and *terephthalic acid*. Systematic names of monomers: butane-1,4-diol and benzene-1,4-dicarboxylic acid 	
PC	polycarbonate 	

Other polymers* continued

abbreviation	names (systematic name - normal type, traditional names - *italic*), structures and comments	example of trade names
PEBA	polyether-block-amide	PEBAX
crosslinked PE	*polyethylene* with crosslinked polymer chains for improved heat-resistance	
PMMA	*poly(methyl methacrylate)* poly(methyl 2-methyl propenoate) 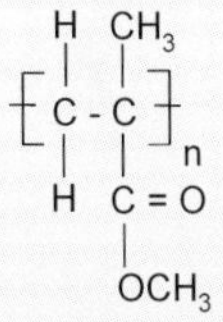 structure of PMMA repeat unit: $\left[CH(H)-C(CH_3)\right]_n$ with side group $C=O$ and OCH_3	Altuglas Plexiglas Perspex
polyaramids	polymers containing the following structure: 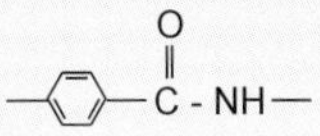 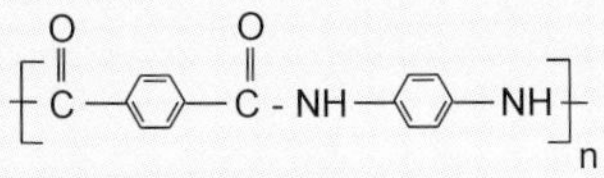 aromatic ring with $-C(O)-NH-$ example Kevlar® structure: $\left[C(O)-\text{(ring)}-C(O)-NH-\text{(ring)}-NH\right]_n$ example Kevlar®	Kevlar®
unsaturated polyesters	polymers with the following groups in 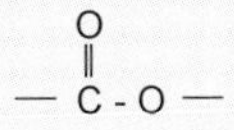 ntheir structures: $-C(O)-O-$ and $-CH=CH-$	
POM	polyacetal	
PPS	polyphenylene sulphide	
PTFE	*polytetrafluoroethylene* poly(tetrafluoroethene) 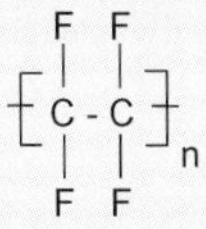 $\left[CF_2-CF_2\right]_n$	Teflon
PU	polyurethanes: polymers with the following groups in their structures: 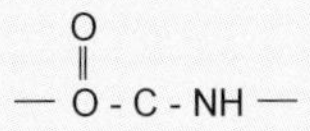 $-O-C(O)-NH-$ NB: monomers, mainly diols and di-isocyanates, generally polymerise during the shaping operation (e.g. when solvents evaporate from paints, or when the two monomers of a polyurethane foam are being injected into a mould)	
chlorinated PVC (C-PVC)	PVC on which extra chlorine atoms have been chemically grafted to improve its flame resistance	Lucalor
PVDC	*polyvinylidene chloride* poly(1,1-dichloroethene) 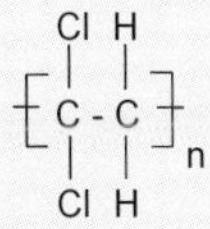 $\left[CCl_2-CH_2\right]_n$	
PVDF	*polyvinylidene fluoride* poly(1,1-difluoroethene) 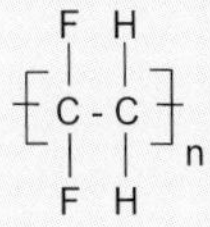 $\left[CF_2-CH_2\right]_n$	Kynar